**You can still make
millions in the
stock market**

You can still make millions in the stock market

SAMUEL MITCHELL

Dow Jones–Irwin
Homewood, Illinois 60430

First Printing, January 1975
Second Printing, May 1976

Printed in the United States of America

Library of Congress Cataloging in Publication Data

Mitchell, Samuel.
    You can still make millions in the stock market.

    1. Investments. 2. Speculation. I. Title.
HG4521.M543   332.6'78   74–18030
ISBN 0-87094-086-4

Preface

If you expect me to disclose a magic formula that will make you a millionaire quickly, read no further, because I will not. Nor will I tell you how to buy low and sell high, use stop-loss orders, go short, buy puts, calls, straddles, or any other gimmicks. I have read advertisements for such systems, but common sense tells me there never was, nor ever will be, a way to turn lead into gold. But if you decide to stay with me for awhile, you will learn how this writer—starting from scratch as an advertising man, not a Wall Street expert —made a profit of some $4 million in less than two decades; and that was not all LUCK.

The purpose of this book is to show the reader, step by step, how I made the millions I did. But the best advice will do you no good until you thoroughly understand that the investment industry does not work the way most people expect it to. The speed and impatience with which we throw our chips on the table indicates one thing to this writer—we honestly think this is an easy way to make a fast buck.

I promise to give you a very honest accounting of what I did *right* to make my few million; and also—and this is most important—what I escaped doing *wrong.*

If experience is still the best teacher, let it be the experience of others.

The subject of losses has become almost a fetish with me, and you will learn the painless way to deal with and avoid them by reading the chapters that deal with losses. Only then will you be able to understand how this novice investor, with very little money to start with

1. Amassed a fortune of $4,000,000.
2. Had losses equaling less than 1 percent.
3. Managed to do it without the use of crystal balls, computers, charts, secret systems, or inside information from the chief operating officer's son or beautiful daughter.

Along the way, I will freely disclose some of my ideas—and you'll find they are contrary to the thinking of most analysts. You will learn that I stay away from CROWDS for very sound reasons. I do not believe in arguing with Success. After all, I must be doing something right—and I have been doing it for a score of years. That is a very good *score.*

Samuel Mitchell

Contents

1. The wailing walls of Wall Street 1
2. The forbidden four letter word. 11
3. The plight of the small investor. 23
4. The plight of the brokers 31
5. Socrates, the great advisor 41
6. Success is spelled M-A-N-A-G-E-M-E-N-T 51
7. Las Vegas 59
8. The truth about tips 65
9. The Khans of Wall Street. 77
10. The devil's seven disciples 83
11. The Wall Street Zoo. 103
12. The subject is asses (or how to save your own). 111
13. The Xerox story 117
14. C. Peter McColough: A continuation of the Xerox
    story 137
15. Summing up 147
Index 153

chapter one

The wailing walls of Wall Street

The root of our problem—the frustrations of the average investor in achieving the success he honestly believes he is entitled to—lies in the fact that most players do not fully understand the kind of game they are playing. This statement may surprise you; actually, it's an understatement of the true facts. Perhaps you will better understand my position if we divide this great investment industry into two parts, theory and practice.

Put yourself in the place of an investment industry trainee who attends a class given by schools and the larger brokerage houses. Here you will learn all about common stocks, preferred stocks, convertible preferred, various bonds—corporate, convertible, callable and noncallable, government, municipal, foreign—government and corporate notes, commercial paper, and so on. You will also learn to analyze corporate annual and interim reports showing sales, expenses, income before taxes, income after taxes, depreciation, write-offs, etcetera. You will learn how to calculate and compare growth rates of various companies in various industries and the price-earnings ratio market valuations. Let's give you an *A* for proficiency and have you pass the tests given by the New York Stock Exchange that allow you to become a registered representative. Now you're in business, as far as *theory* is concerned.

The second part of the problem is the matter of practice—the practical use of our knowledge and our own money—which, we must concede, is relatively more important than our proficiency in theory. And here is where the ruthless finger of fate separates the boys from the men and we discover, much to our surprise and chagrin, that practically all of us are living in a boy's world. And all this time we thought we, of all people, should be considered professionals! In this day of instant communications, a wealth of statistical data concerning all the publicly held corporations is available to novice and professional alike. Shouldn't it be a very simple matter for the novice or professional investor or adviser to get this information and come to some conclusion as to whether he should buy or sell a certain stock, providing he limits his studies to a few issues? It really *is* a simple matter, as I shall demonstrate later.

Some investors may feel that the professional has a decided advantage over the novice even though they both have access to the same set of statistics, since the pro can avail himself of charts and electronic tools of the trade that measure the upticks and downticks throughout the day, the volume accompanying each tick, thereby determining whether the stock is being accumulated or distributed—by the insiders, I suppose. I have always disagreed with this kind of ultimate conclusion, and when some of the salesmen who try to sell me any of these systems graciously concede that I am entitled to "one man's opinion," I remind them that this man's opinion has a back-log of profits totaling several million dollars. I am old-fash-ioned, I presume, when I contend that a fisherman with the newest and most expensive tackle doesn't necessarily catch the most fish; the barefoot boy using a line and a bent pin may give him a run for his money.

I have no desire to underrate professionalism. There are plenty of lessons to be learned from the pros. Occasionally, an investor buys a stock by pure chance and makes a huge profit, and he forevermore boasts about his skill as a stock analyst. Face it. That's dumb luck—the same kind of luck you run into in the game of golf, when the world's worst duffer makes a miraculous shot. I actually played with a friend some years ago who shanked his shot about a mile off target. It struck a tree, caromed 50 yards onto the green, and almost dropped in for an eagle. He too never stopped talking about it. In sharp contrast, I witnessed Jack Nicklaus in deep trou-ble on the 17th hole of an important match. His second shot hit an incline to the right of the green and bounded behind some trees. Losing that hole would probably have cost him the tournament. Somehow, he exploded a shot through the trees and dropped the ball two feet from the pin. Luck? Oh no! Skill, a careful reading of the situation, and letting go with the kind of shot experience told him to use.

Watching Jack Nicklaus or Arnold Palmer or any of the greats, using the same golf clubs they do, wearing the same style slacks will never make a pro out of a duffer, any more than reading how J. Paul Getty made a billion or so will help you make a mountain of gold out of a molehill of kopecks. But having a golf pro point out all your faults will surely help improve your game. In our little game of portfolio management, I say most emphatically that *to become a successful investor, you must take careful note of how and why LOSSES occur and how stockpiling losses destroys once-rich and profitable holdings.*

And that brings us to another very important lesson. Although you must learn about losses, they don't have to be your own losses for the message to sink in. I find it much less painful to study my colleagues' losses than to make mistakes myself. All it takes to audit a postgraduate course in losses, errors, mistakes, and—most importantly—how to avoid them, is a visit to the Wailing Walls of Wall Street.

For active participants, the Wailing Walls of Wall Street are erected spontaneously whenever investors who've sustained significant losses meet to bemoan their fate and console themselves. Personally, I cannot vouch for the consolation to be found there. I recommend a visit to any current Wailing Wall for a very valid learning experience. When I go, I interview the mourners. I want to find out what really happened, the habits of the bereaved, why they bought certain stocks, and what the coroner has to say about the company management responsible for the catastrophe. That is the best way I know to learn by other people's mistakes. They say experience is the best teacher; better still are other people's experiences where losses are concerned. There is no doubt that the Wailing Walls have kept my personal losses in the market down to subminimum.

Here's what happened on a visit to the Levitz Furniture

Wailing Wall. I am not selecting Levitz by hindsight. Actually, I knew there would be a Wailing Wall for Levitz long before the stock collapsed. I met a number of investors at the Wailing Wall who bemoaned the fact that they never got in when the price was low. Several of my own clients howled when I did not buy Levitz for them. One actually left my portfolio management service and went to another adviser— who did put him in. There he was at the Wall. And then there were some investors who went short when the stock was much lower. Most of the mourners, however, had gotten sucked in by accepting the Levitz operation at face value, never thinking to ask themselves some very important questions about what really existed behind the glamour. Stripped of all the excitement, here are the facts that were available to those who bought Levitz—and to those of us who didn't:

The Levitz people sold branded furniture and lower quality reproductions at low warehouse–direct-to-you prices.

The Levitz people were experienced furniture men and agressive promoters.

They expanded very rapidly, opening up large warehouses in areas that were growing just as rapidly, population-wise.

Doubling their warehouses brought sales, and also doubled earnings, almost in a routine manner.

Management kept releasing glowing predictions of future sales and earnings (which I personally thought unwise at the time).

Meantime, Levitz stock kept going higher and higher, splitting and continuing to hit new highs; it went above $60 a share, which represented a price-earnings ratio of 80 to 100.

P/E of 80–100

Had Levitz stockholders asked themselves the same questions I did when I made my decision on the stock, they would have come to the same conclusions that I did.

Shelving the apparent Levitz expertise that enabled them to get a big jump on their competitors, has Levitz any patent rights to do what other large furniture retailers cannot do?

Can Levitz buy for less than other furniture dealers with similar or larger buying power?

Can Levitz pay less rent, pay their buyers less, make a better deal with the unions than their competitors?

Can Levitz buy time on TV and radio and space in the local newspapers for less?

Over the long run, can Levitz sell for less without running into the red?

The answer to all of these questions is, of course, NO! Not for the long run, because competitors stay awake nights trying to keep ahead of you. Then why should I, as an investor, pay such a high price/earnings premium to own a piece of Levitz when I can invest in other furniture merchants at 12 times earnings? Or if I want to stay away from furniture, I can buy some very sound dividend-paying stocks in the Dow Jones averages that sell for less than 12 times earnings.

Almost overnight, Levitz dropped from $60 to $30. It took a bit longer to drop to $30, $20, to $10, and then to $4 by Thanksgiving Day 1973, which was no fault of Levitz's since the Dow Jones dropped almost 150 points. Let us all be thankful we could afford turkey.

I mention Levitz in such great detail only to show my readers the kind of thinking that has kept me away from losses for the past two decades—that kept me out of the bowling stocks, the overpriced conglomerates, the fast food franchises, and many other respectable companies that fared worse than Levitz—some declining from highs of $150 and more to less than the dividends they once paid.

In my experience, the most valuable knowledge you can apply to the stock market is to explore, examine, and evaluate a company *before* you acquire a piece of it. There are thousands of companies listed on the major exchanges and available in the over-the-counter markets. Vital statistics relating to past and current sales, earnings, dividends, and so on are available for all these companies. And there are countless customer's men, analysts, advisers, and advisory services ready to supply you with the information you need to make well-informed judgments.

I have tried to apply a simple, commonsense approach to *acquiring* stock. I try to examine each stock on its own merits without the hindrance of any preconceived notions. This simple approach is not too prevalent among investors—Much too often, I have found that the hasty always-in-a-hurry compulsive traders haven't the foggiest notion why they buy a stock other than (I quote) "to make some money."

You will note that I use the term *acquiring*. In effect, when you become a shareowner, you are *acquiring* a piece of another man's business and, as such, you should consider it in the proper perspective. Why do you want a piece of that particular business? You must have a reason. Do you want to hold it long term or are you buying it for a quick turn? In either event, if you know what you are doing, you will want to learn something about the company.

If you were an investor with great wealth or the guiding light of a large fund or institution, how would you go about acquiring a piece of another man's business? You would naturally assemble all the vital statistics about the company over a period of years:

> Total operating revenues
> Net income before and after taxes
> Depreciation of plant and equipment
> Amortization of patents
> Income from subsidiaries
> Cash and marketable securities
> Current assets
> Current liabilities
> Cash flow
> Long-term debts
> Shareholders' equity

You would also gather comparable statistics on that company's competitors and the industry itself.

Apart from these fundamentals is the consistency of the company's growth and the competence of its management. To this end, you would have your man Friday or your bank visit the company, speak to the management, learn where it is heading: their plans for research, product improvement, and new product development; personnel and production expansion plans; possible acquisitions; new financing; and so forth. A thorough study of all these factors together with the market action of the stock over a like period of years should result in a fairly accurate evaluation of what the stock is really worth. Of course, you are probably shouting at this point, "I am one person, and all I can afford to do is acquire a little piece of a few companies via a modest stock portfolio. How can I afford to visit each company that interests me and dig out all this information?" I will let you in on one of my most important secrets: This is the very formula I follow with every stock I acquire for myself or for the people whose portfolios I manage, and if I cannot make the exploration physically, I can *always* make it mentally. The facts are in the public domain. A broker can get data into your hands in a matter of hours or days. A variety of advisers is available to lead you by the hand if you don't feel competent to evaluate the information on your own—especially at the start. If you don't take the time to explore, examine, and evaluate, you won't be just an observer at the Wailing Wall. You'll be a frequent participant.

A best selling book compared investing to a game. Some people talk about playing the market. If playing the market is a game, then most assuredly it is a very serious game, one that requires great skill. It doesn't matter how you have accumulated the money you want to invest. The failure of your investments can destroy a lifetime's accumulation. Go to the Wailing Wall to learn. What you'll learn is that it is worth taking a second look *before* you leap . . . and perhaps a third look too.

chapter two

The forbidden four letter word

Walk along a beach in July, go into any movie house in New York's Times Square, open a book on the bestseller list, and you'll be convinced we live in a wide-open society. It seems a bit unnatural that in our sophisticated world, a certain four letter word is still forbidden on Wall Street and that cults, sects, taboos, and superstitions still exist there. A cult of silence persists whenever the investment industry is confronted with the four letter word spelled L O S S, and frankly I am at a loss to explain why nobody ever uses it when discussing the extent of his profits. You may be unaware that you are an involuntary member of this cult, but the truth is that you are, unless you come out courageously and use it in your daily conversations. Don't fall prey to that oldie, *Silence is golden.* Let others talk about your profits; you do your talking about your losses until you learn how to *avoid* them.

If you can share some of my fascination with that four letter word, loss, you will understand why I did so well with my investments. Please note that the Greeks had a word, *luein,* meaning to loosen; and the Latin *lues* meant plague, pestilence, to loosen, divide, cut apart—such as *to lose one's balance; to fail to hear, see, or understand; to lose oneself* as from everyday reality; *to lose one's way; to disappear* or *fade away; to lose one's way in a crowd; to suffer a loss* as in buying a stock for $100 and selling it for $25. This last touch I added; the rest are quotes from my dictionary, yet they sound as though they refer to our investments.

Like many a poor boy who became rich, I can also say I never attended a college of finance. My guess is that the Harvard Business School does not have a course devoted to losses; and if it ever starts one, I would like to suggest the following test question:

> You are given an unlimited amount of money and told to bet $1,000 on red at the roulette table. You lose the first bet and must double your bet on the next round. You keep betting and losing each time, $2,000, $4,000, $8,000, $16,000, $32,000, $64,000, and $128,-000. On the next bet you finally win. How much do you win?

I urge you to take this test. Take your pencil and pad and figure it out. In the meantime, let me relate a story that is pertinent. (Thanks to my pal, Henny Youngman.)

A compulsive gambler on basketball games kept his bookie busy and prosperous by betting every game the bookie could find. After a few weeks betting on a half a hundred or more basketball games—and losing every bet he made—he called his bookie and asked, "How many basketball games today?"

The bookie replied, "No basketball games today, but there are two hockey games."

"What do I know about hockey?" cried the compulsive gambler.

It would not be a bad idea if we sophisticated investors would pause after a long dry spell of losses on every stock we bought to ask ourselves that same question: "What do I know about stocks?"

Here is the answer to the test question; compare it with your own.

> You would collect $512,000 on your last bet. But, you will have wagered in all a total of $511,000. You would wind up winning $1,000 net; that is, if you didn't suffer a heart attack on the way.

Doesn't this test question remind you of some of the hustle and bustle that goes on among some traders? They are in and out, a profit here, a profit there, a little loss here, and a much bigger loss there. At the end of the quarter they total their profits and subtract their losses and all the buy and sell commissions; more often than not, the bottom line shows a net loss or, at best, a decidedly puny profit.

Fortunately, I learned my lesson when I first started to conquer Wall Street and all I had to invest was a few hundred dollars. It took some time for me to draw the conclusion that losses were somewhat like the atom bomb. An understandable degree of fear and secrecy surrounds both of them. Until the first atom bomb was dropped on Hiroshima, complete silence surrounded the scientists who were working on the project. The Japanese, too, were silent about their atomic bomb project. Fortunately for our own survival, the United States got there first. After the Japanese surrendered, the Americans found a nearly completed cyclotron atom smasher in Japan; it was taken out to sea and sunk.

You can't put your investment losses in a box and sink them in the ocean, but you can learn from them. Rather than join the silent majority that keeps quiet about losses, look a loss straight in the face. Find out how it happened. You may learn a thing or two that will surprise you. One thing you'll learn is that the word *loss* sounds a lot like the word *lesson,* and a successful investor learns his lesson the first time.

Take a lesson from Willie Mays. Willie Mays was a natural, one of the greatest ball players of all time, not only as a homerun hitter, but as an RBI hitter, a base stealer, a fielder, and a thrower. Yet, tops that he was, he never missed practice and he and his coaches were *always alert to detect and correct anything that he might be doing wrong.* That is the hallmark of success.

It is easy enough for me to tell you what I did right. My accountant can show you a statement of what I bought, at what price, and if I sold or still hold it. But that won't help you any; you cannot turn back the clock and match what I bought and sold; nor can you buy what the Rothschilds did. You must be alert to what you have been doing wrong. What I *can* do, now that we've managed to get the word *loss* out in the open, is point out to you a lot of things that perhaps you did—which resulted in some of your losses.

Back in 1968 the market was booming. Everybody I knew was making a barrel of money buying new issues that doubled in value before they hit the market. I didn't buy any of them because to me it was the wrong thing to do. The conglomerates were having a field day; they would offer $30 a share for a stock that was selling at $15, and overnight the $15 stock ran up to the tender price and the conglomerate gobbled it up. Meantime, everybody started buying the conglomerates as well, the moment a tender-takeover or merger was hinted. It was all wrong, as far as I could see when I went looking for the prospective earnings that would warrant such high P/E multiples. I stayed away from a great number of stocks that were skyrocketing—some with the help of go-go fund managers who were often responsible for pushing them up. My friends told me that I could have made a bundle taking quick short-term profits; by hindsight, that's true. It's wrong if you start believing that you can be that smart. I don't have to mention the various issues that went down the drain. If you owned any of them, you know which they are—and must now fully realize that unless you first learn what you are doing wrong, you will never improve your batting average.

I have observed through the years that most investors joyfully accept profits on their investments as a matter of course and never stop to consider why these stocks are going up. There are no complaints, no inquiries, no investigations. When the Dow Jones Industrial Average takes a sharp drop and individual issues drop even further percentagewise, a wild cry is heard in the land. Complaints abound—complaints about wrongdoings; complaints about manipulations that make the insiders rich and the suckers poorer; complaints about conflicts of interest, churning, and downright swindles. Here and there an insider is fined, a swindler flees the country or is jailed before he can get away . . . all of which, by the way, affect institutional as well as individual investors.

In a bullish climate, however, very few animal lovers give a second thought to the forgotten bears. They might be coming out of hibernation, lean and hungry. Such, I imagine, was their condition during the closing months of 1968. It should not have been difficult for the average analyst to foresee what would happen if they ever broke loose. A hungry bear is a dangerous bear.

Not too surprisingly, the first stocks the bears reach and gobble up are the high-flying volatile issues. The financial writers watch the feast and *attempt to* tell us why the market is going down in these words:

1. Profit-taking.
2. The institutions are selling.
3. Lower earnings anticipated.
4. A big loss anticipated versus a big profit the year before.
5. Incoming orders decline.
6. Expansion plans cancelled.
7. Merger discussions terminated.
8. Money is tight and interest rates are soaring.
9. Big corporations are having liquidity trouble.
10. The cost of living is rising.
11. Unemployment is rising.
12. Profit margins are tightening.
13. Proxy fights.
14. Brokerage houses are in financial trouble.
15. Etcetera, etcetera, etcetera.

These reasons are given *after* the decline and *after* the close of the market—a day after, a week after, or a month after, but always after the *fait accompli*. And after the averages have dropped for awhile, your friendly adviser adds (if he is like many customers' men I know), "They're going lower; you haven't seen bottom yet. Sell! Notwithstanding, they tout XYZ. Buy XYZ and you'll make back your losses." Why don't some of them warn us a day before it happens?

Fortunately, it is not very difficult for anyone to see for himself how his stocks did, as well as how all other stocks behaved. The only requirements are good eyesight, the ability to read English and the money to buy a copy of the *Wall Street Journal.*

Because he's associated with Wall Street's forbidden four letter word, the poor bear is generally despised among investment professionals. Not by me! I find one bear quite lovable; in my book, he's the best friend an investor ever had. Whereas even a stuffed Kodiak bear scares the hell out of me, I am quite chummy with Smokey the Bear—and for a very good reason.

Every child knows Smokey and his admonition: "Only *you* can prevent forest fires." I want you to substitute the words *"stock losses"* for *"forest fires,"* and you will understand why Smokey and I are such pals. It's the simple things in life that often escape us. If you stop playing with matches, you will never start a fire—nor have a loss in a volatile stock.

For me to show you how to stop playing with fire and how to correct your mistakes, memorize the following rules.

1. *Change your ways.* If you have been picking stocks yourself and stockpiling losses during a bull market, what makes you think you can make money in a bear market? Unless you can change your ways, put your money in AAA bonds and quit trading. Bill Demarest, the golf pro, on Johnny Carson's Tonight Show, gave Johnny this bit of advice: "Lay off for a few weeks, Johnny, and then quit."

2. *Don't play with fire.* A baby, crawling on all fours, learns this lesson: "Hot, hot," says mama as baby reaches for

the radiator; but after the baby touches it just once, he has learned to keep away. Are grownups any smarter? A stock gets hot, which means it doubles or triples in price overnight. No one asks *why?* Thousands upon thousands jump on the band wagon and get cremated.

3. *Be on the lookout for smoke signals.* Your house is always in danger of fire when your neighbor's house starts to burn. Even the slightest sparks must not fly unnoticed. Watch your own portfolio of stocks when your neighbors' hot issues begin to sputter.

4. *Be on the alert even though the sky is clear.* Every bear market is preceded and caused by a bull market. When your investment portfolio is jam-packed with profits, put on your fire inspector's hat and check over all your holdings. There may be some volatile stocks (rubbish) that should be cleaned out before they ignite. And if they have resisted the downtrend, don't make the mistake of thinking *all* your holdings are immune. Re-evaluate them as thoroughly as you would if you were ready to make a new investment.

5. *Never go from hot to hotter.* As a bullish market starts peaking out, a great many stocks begin outperforming your own holdings. There is a great temptation to switch to some high-riding favorites. If you look carefully, you will find those dark clouds of uncertainty are really smoke signals that precede the forest fire. The all-consuming bear market may be closer than you think. As individual stocks become over-priced, the hibernating bears begin to awaken. Rather then move into some-

thing more volatile, switch into cash and put it in a fireproof vault.

6. *Smokey says, "Keep your cool."* Don't get overly excited about the big blaze over the hill; don't rush over and forget to put out the small fire in your own backyard. To many investors, the sight of a onetime favorite that sold as high as $170 dropping to $85 in a very short time seems to signal that the fire is over and it is a wonderful buy. Don't start counting your profits and anticipating when it will return to $170. Instead, get yourself an expert (fire prevention) appraiser to evaluate the smouldering ruins.

7. *Short can be hot.* The opportunist's dilemma: The forest fire is in full blast. Some predict the worst is over; others believe it will spread still further. The Wall Street trader (fire fighter) is getting tired, weary, worrisome. All his stocks are down, dangerously close to getting a margin call. In contrast to his own weariness, he meets a very talkative and extremely self-satisfied neighbor who has been shorting stocks willy nilly and taking some very quick profits. Here is evidence that you can make money in a bear market, or so it seems. It always surprises me to learn that so many succumb and go short—willy nilly—even though the stocks they pick to short have already declined 50% or more. I have added the words willy-nilly because I have observed that these latecomers to the shorters never bother to evaluate the companies they are shorting, nor to compare their futures with those of other sisters in distress. Obviously, they feel that the deeper a stock falls, the

futher it will continue to fall. A bear market is *never* a bottomless pit.

8. *It can be smarter to sit than switch.* This is an age-old problem common to bull markets as well as bear markets. You're beginning to lose interest in the stock you're married to and are seriously considering switching to a stock with more excitement. Evaluate—the old and the new—but remember if you decide to switch it will cost you money in double and triple commissions and taxes on your profits.

[handwritten margin notes: switching : Double Commissions + TAXES]

9. *Better be alone than in bad company.* I found this bit of wisdom in a chinese fortune cookie. The average trader will prevent many losses if he follows this bit of advice. There is something in the investment operation that brings out the impatience in man, and always when caution tells you to stay home. Why should an investor be in such a hurry to buy something the moment he sells a stock? Expert bridge players have a great deal of respect for the bid, "Pass." The poor bridge player seldom passes; it is difficult for him to keep quiet, even with a worthless hand. Similarly, the consistent loser hates to pass up a worthless speculation.

10. *Where's the fire?* This rather common query is used by traffic cops and state troopers when they stop you for driving beyond the speed limit. One gagster asked a state trooper how many cars he had stopped that day with the same query. When he replied, "About a dozen," the driver said, "And you still don't know where the fire is?" Unfortunately, the trooper had no sense of humor. I lose my own sense of humor when

I see my friends rushing to buy a hot new issue at about a hundred or two hundred times earnings yet unborn. You would think they were getting in at fire-sale prices. The only thing burning, I am convinced, is the money in the sucker's pocket.

11. *Don't become envious when all about you are boasting of the quick profits they are making.* I heard them daily in 1968. "I just made $20,000," a young lodge brother of mine reported. By the middle of May 1970, he came to my office for help. From a peak of over $40,000, his bunch of garbage was worth less than $1,500.

12. *"To thine own self be true,"* and *"self-deception succumbs to self-destruction."* The first quotation comes from Shakespeare; the second is another bit of Taoist wisdom from the teachings of Lao Tzu, 600 B.C. Both have a profound affect on the success or failure of your investment practices. Translated into today's English, they mean *don't kid yourself.* The moment you take full credit for a profit you made and hide the fact that it was really someone else's doing, you may be heading toward self-destruction.

chapter three

The plight of the small investor

Every now and then, in good times or bad—but mostly when the market averages drop, even for a day—financial writers say the little man is out of the market. Some state rather authoritively that the small investor is being forced out of the market. A staff writer for a Los Angeles paper wrote about a small investor who bought some Occidental Petroleum when it spurted after the published news item that Occidental made a deal with the Soviet Union involving a few billion dollars. The stock dropped sharply after he bought it, and he took a big loss. On another occasion, the same investor sold AT & T warrants *short* at around $5 and covered when it went to $9, taking another loss. And now this little investor is out of the market—indicating, I suppose, that the market is no place for the small fellow. I disagree!

I certainly hold no brief for the stock market, although it

made this once-small investor a millionaire several times over. But to hold the stock market responsible for the losses suffered by misguided investors who have a knack for doing everything wrong shows a very poor understanding of the investment business. Of course, the plight of the small investor is real, not fancied. My aim in discussing his plight fully is to demonstrate that despite the inequities of the brokerage business and (perhaps) the inadequacies of the individual, the small investor can succeed in this most difficult of businesses.

In our usage, *little man* does not refer to an individual's stature nor to the amount of his wealth, but rather to the size of the transaction he is considering at the moment. We old retailers have all seen a new customer who appears to be broke and simply in search of a trinket of little value; yet, treated courteously by the sales clerk, he turns out to be a man of great wealth. On the other hand, many a man of good appearance, commanding great respect and attention as he inquires about the price of the most expensive item in the store, turns out to be what we euphamistically call a phony.

At one time, large brokerage houses encouraged their people to woo small investors, hoping eventually to build them into large accounts. This was the success formula in all businesses. This is *not* the accepted practice today. How the little man is being treated, I am sure, must eventually effect the destiny of the broker. As a case in point, I would like to relate the history of one of this country's great retail institutions, Best & Co.

Here was a Fifth Avenue fashion store that, in the midst of the stiffest competition, earned the highest percentage profit on sales year after year. Good financial analysts pay a great deal of attention to any company that can maintain a higher margin of profit than its competitors. What is more important to me is who in management is responsible for such consistent profits. Long before I had achieved success in the stock market, I evaluated the management of retail fashion institutions in connection with my advertising and marketing service. At Best & Co., Mr. Phillip le Boutelier was the man—the owner and guiding spirit. I met him several times to discuss some ideas of mine. He was most cordial and, in spite of his affluence, he made me feel important. On one occasion, when I was ready to leave he helped me on with my coat and walked with me to the elevator—the perfect host. I found this to be an indication of how he wanted his customers to be treated as well. I happened to be in the store one day and witnessed Mr. le Boutelier walking over to a woman. She had a minor complaint that could have been handled by any clerk, but because he was there, he took care of it himself. I also learned that the eager garment manufacturers' salesmen who descended upon the Best & Co. buyers in droves were treated with the same respect and consideration that Best & Co. customers and shoppers received. The Best & Co. label was more than a mark of quality merchandise; it was a classic symbol of public relations at its "Best."

In recent years, Best & Co. and its 14 branch stores were taken over by a corporation that owned and operated a large chain of retail stores. Remote corporate management could never replace the personal customer relationship le Boutelier had founded and nurtured. It was quite a shock to oldtimers (though not to me) when Best & Co. announced later that it was closing its doors. A half-price sale drew great crowds.

Said one shopper, "This isn't Best & Co. anymore. It looks like. . . ." (She said the name of another store better known for its lower prices than for its quality.)

Is the demise of Best & Co. a subtle warning to our great brokerage institutions not to underestimate the value of service? Could very well be, judging by the complaints of the little investors about how they are being treated. For a better understanding of the little investor's plight and how he can improve his lot, let's briefly review what has been going on concerning the subject of brokerage commissions or fees, which the brokerage house needs to keep financially well fed.

After months of discussions and study by the stock exchanges, who represented their brokerage house members, the institutions, who buy and sell large blocks of securities, and the Securities and Exchange Commission, a schedule of negotiated commissions was arrived at. A large institution is now allowed to shop around and negotiate with a number of member brokerage houses for a lower than fixed commission on its block transactions. The little fellow, of course, cannot do so; and if the day comes when he can, I strongly advise him not to waste his time. (I'll give my reasons in a subsequent chapter.)

I am not debating the merits of negotiated commissions. Large buyers *are* entitled to special privileges and discounts. Even a case of liquor costs the drinker less per bottle, though in my own case, since I drink very slowly, the storage charges plus interest on my investment would negate my original savings.

However, to meet the mounting costs of operating a brokerage house, lowered negotiated commissions may not be sufficient to maintain the staff of analysts and salesmen needed to get the business. The anticipated deficit had to be made up—by increasing the commissions the little fellow has to pay on the smallest transactions. This, too, makes good sense, provided this higher commission includes *better* service. Unfortunately, it does not. In some instances the registered representative—the man who has a three-fold responsibility to advise, to sell, and to service his client—actually receives as compensation a *smaller* percentage of the *higher* commission now in effect. On some minimum transactions, he receives nothing. I cannot understand this at all. I would certainly question my boss if he asked me to do more work for less pay than I did before, especially in an inflationary economy.

In Robert Metz's column in *The New York Times,* I read of one dedicated registered representative who spent hours selecting five different stocks to go into a $5,000 portfolio for a new client. His total take-home pay amounted to about $10. The only fringe benefit he could expect was having to answer the torrent of phone calls that would surely follow asking why stock A or B was off a quarter of a point. On the other hand, a less conscientious RR can easily persuade a similar client to invest in a mutual fund. About all he has to say is, "Let them do the worrying for you. That's what they're paid for." Sounds very convincing. Better for the house, too, which receives $350 commission and gives the RR $175.

Better for the small investor? Of course not! But what is the little fellow to do? I've just told you that there's good reason for the RR *not* to have your best interests at heart. Should you stop buying stocks entirely? No. You will find many suggestions in later chapters for confronting the whole scope of the stock-investing situation, but as for how to handle the specific instance I just mentioned, ask the RR who suggests mutual funds to pick a no-load fund. That means the fund does not charge you an 8½% sales load that goes to pay the commissions to the brokers. Otherwise, if you put $1,000 into a mutual fund, $915 worth of stock is all you actually get. It may eventually prove to be a good investment, but you should know at the outset that you're starting off with an 8½% loss!

The message here is that *you cannot be too well informed!* Wall Street fishermen have noted from time to time that a barefoot novice in tattered jeans will hook onto a little-known stock and make a fortune, usually in some area that the more sophisticated investor won't give a second glance. Actually, this is the exception that proves the rule—and the rule is that the pro who studies the seas and the currents to discover where and when the fish are likely to bite will catch more fish.

To bring my reader's financial know-how into sharper focus, I will detail *every* step of the way in the following chapters—from the time you first hear of a stock to the point at which you decide to buy it, sell it or hold it, to take a profit, a loss, or to let it ride.

I must take you into my confidence. You may note, as you go along with me, that I go to great lengths to illustrate a simple point; in fact, you may criticize me for so doing. But there is a purpose in my madness. I am deliberately trying to slow you up, for if there is one place where you should take you time, it is the security business. I say this emphatically because if I were asked to pinpoint the one reason why so many investors go broke, I would say, "They're in a hurry.

They can't wait to get rich. They always want to know what they can buy *now*, this minute!" Some investors cannot wait to find out the correct name of the company or what it does. You probably have heard of the customer who calls his broker to buy a hundred shares of a certain stock. He's not sure of the company's name or what it does, but he's heard the stock's hot—and he wants in before it cools. These traders should heed my advice: Don't put off until tomorrow what you can buy just as well next week.

chapter four

The plight of the brokers

The butcher, the baker, and the candlestick maker had to know their business in order to survive. The extent of their success depended to a large degree on their abilities, their labors, and their personalities. The same golden rule governs us all in our various vocations and avocations. All of which is, of course, an oversimplification of the plight of the brokers today. But the plight of the small investor—in fact of *all* investors—is inexorably tied to the plight of the brokers, so we can profit from a thorough understanding of exactly what the brokers' problems are.

It was not uncommon to hear gagsters a half-century ago, viewing a yacht basin filled with ocean-going yachts, say: "Oh, they belong to the Wall Street brokers, and those little rowboats scurrying about belong to their customers." The present picture is entirely different, and it's a picture that is frightening in its implications, even to this unshakable optimist. The ghastly specter of the grim reaper of October 1929 was reported in our midst in 1969, and it turned out not to be just an apparition. Only this time the customers were not alone floundering in their tiny boats and rafts or frantically reaching for a life preserver drifting by; the yachts were in trouble too.

Brokerage houses, large and small, were having their own headaches. Members of the New York Stock Exchange, whose financial status was always thought to be inviolate, were losing money perhaps *faster* than customers. No one, it seems, was prepared for such an eventuality. We little fellows were kept in the dark, not by design, I am sure, but through force of habit. How were we supposed to be able to evaluate what was going on, to pinpoint the reasons for the Dow Jones averages hitting new lows for such a long period of time? Projected earnings estimates weren't that bad, particularly for the 30 stocks that comprise the Dow Jones averages. Here and there happenings would hit the broadtape news tickers and the market panicked; in retrospect, I contend the market averages should have fared worse.

Just one shock at a time: The great Penn Central Railroad, the largest in the world, pleaded with the government for a loan to help meet its payrolls. Highly trusted companies estimated earnings of $15 a share. When the loan was refused, Penn Central filed for bankruptcy. The stock plummeted to several dollars a share. Even our most astute bankers were stuck with tens of millions of dollars worth of the Penn's commercial paper.

On another fair day (without a dark cloud in sight) Henry Ross Perot's Electronic Data Systems collapsed, and his personal holding dropped almost a half billion dollars in market value. Bernard Cornfeld's Investors Overseas Services dropped some $75 million in bad investments in six months and we all watched his stock sink from $20 to about $3 in the same time period. Ling, Temco, Vought dropped from $170 two years earlier to $16. And there were others, like Memorex and University Computing, that also peaked at the magic $170 price, only to fare even worse.

It was not surprising that each incident added to the woes of the brokerage houses. Back-office traffic jams and mounting expenses coupled with declining volume into one-two punches that the securities industry was in no condition to absorb. Lower volume at lower prices greatly reduced income, so the authorities imposed a $15 surcharge on each transaction to help remedy the situation—for the broker. Come to think of it, it might not be a bad idea if the government would grant me a bonus or subsidy every time I buy or sell a stock—win, lose, or draw. *That* certainly would encourage trading.

While the averages continued to hit new lows, ominous hints abounded: One broker fired the entire research staff (they are usually the first to leave—unless you include the clients; going out of the business is next, unless some sort of face-saving merger is arranged). Good old names like Goodbody & Co. vanished. "What's in a name?" asked Shakespeare. In this particular name 225,000 accounts placed their trust. Then, in a crisis-filled climate fearfully approaching a climax, came the news that the iron-clad investment firm of Francis I. du Pont was in even deeper financial trouble. In 1969, it was third largest brokerage house in the country, behind Merrill Lynch and Bache. I don't think the public, by and large, knew too much about what was going on at the time, and perhaps that's just as well, for this was the brink of disaster. Very fortunately, we survived that particular brink with the aid of a rescue fund the New York Stock Exchange its members wisely set up and a massive blood infusion from some outsiders.

Those were the horror headlines, but the momentous problems that beset the brokerage houses are far from solved. Where it all leads to, no one can say at this point. We will have to find a solution with honor—one in which the brokerage house will make a profit without impairing the health of its customers.

In our search for a solution, let us examine another industry that had comparable problems, the airlines. In their infancy, the airlines had great difficulty selling their services to a public that was afraid to fly. Only the young and courageous risked their lives, plus a few top-level men of industry whose precious time was too costly to be wasted on slower, more leisurely means of transportation.

Some brilliant public relations men came up with an idea that proved to be the turning point. They introduced stewardesses to accompany the passengers to their destinations and look after their comforts. This innovation was an instantaneous success, not unlike the old Times Square sight-seeing bus strategy: The company hired an attractive young lady to sit in the middle of the bus on the side facing the street. The bus speedily filled up with eager young men who had a sudden urge to see the sights of little old New York. Just as the bus was ready to start, the young lady quietly left. The stewardesses, of course, were not so flighty; they stayed on the plane and performed their duties well. A pillow behind your neck was sheer comfort; a second or third glass of your favorite drink was not hard to take either.

As short business trips by air became increasingly popular, and when lonely wives grew suspiciously interested, the airlines instituted half-fares for the wives if they accompanied their husbands. Half-fares were also accorded daughters, who sometimes appeared overly attentive to their daddies. And the airlines began to prosper. But air travel was still in its infancy.

As air travel became commonplace, the planes grew bigger, faster, and safer—and distances became shorter. At the same time, competition grew taller and profits smaller. Enter the same old profit squeeze that confronts the brokerage houses today, and for the same reason—rates (commissions) were fixed by governmental agencies. How the airlines tried to solve their problems may give the brokerage industry some new ideas to ponder.

The B.C. sales plan was updated. (B.C. stands for Beauty and Comfort, two very successful selling points.) The airlines added gourmet menus prepared by disciples of the great Escoffier. First class passengers were feted with champagne, caviar, demi-poule Negresco. The idea mushroomed. To meet competition, menus featured fillet of fresh turbot flown in from the North Sea and poached in court bouillon. Soon we were wolfing down filet mignon bernaise from Maxim's, osso bucco milanese, and Iranian caviar like black diamonds on ice. We never had it so good, and all without extra charge. Airline traffic increased—and so did expenses—but the individual profit picture continued mixed and sluggish. So inflight movies were introduced, certainly an added attraction, but a very confusing one. Now we find it more difficult than ever to choose an airline when we arrange our travel itinerary. When you make arrangements for your vacation this year, you'll probably end up telling your wife, "Dear, on the ninth, Pan Am is serving prime ribs of beef or Dover sole and they're showing a Clark Gable revival. TWA has duck à l'orange, but we've seen the movie. Listen, if we could postpone it until the 10th, TWA is showing a preview of a Swedish movie called 'Confessions of a Nymphomaniac'. . . ."

The problems of an investor are relatively the same as those of the airline passenger, and both are made even more complex by the rate structure. The rate you pay for your plane flight is governed by the location of your seat as well as its width, the latter being of greater import to passengers with larger rear ends. If you choose to ride first class, your fare is considerably more than second class or tourist, whose seat may be directly behind the first-class passenger and may measure an inch or two less in width. Even in the old West, travel on the stage coach had first-class, second-class, and third-class fares. This made absolutely no sense to me, since they only carried five or six passengers, but it was explained by an oldtimer: When a stage coach reached an almost impassable part of the terrain, the first-class passenger remained seated, the second-class got out and walked, and the third-class got out and pushed.

The great institution called Wall Street has a problem strikingly similar to the airlines'. In a sense, the brokerage houses' problem has to do with transportation too. Actually, in our investments, we are daily transporting money through various channels. The consumer pays a small charge for this service; it is called a commission. This charge is calculated on the price of the stock and the number of shares transported. The charge is the same, no matter which carrier gets the business.

Though it may not be apparent at first glance, this is the major stumbling block. The brokerage houses have to make money to stay in business and the investor must also make money to stay in business. Their interests may not always coincide, nor may their intentions.

Any investor has the problem of choosing a brokerage house that will make more money for him. The brokerage house, on the other hand, has the problem of getting enough customers and doing enough business to cover its overhead and make a profit. The "new business" sales managers cannot offer half-price trial specials and the standard pretty-girl approach is of little advantage.

It is extremely simple economics that when the price of a commodity or a service is fixed, the buyer inherits the problem of where to spend his money. And the seller has the task not only of finding the buyer but of convincing him that it is to his advantage to choose him. Bikini-clad coeds cavorting on the Florida sands or Hawaiian hula dancers or wildly gyrating grass-skirted Tahitians may increase your urge to travel, but they don't make it any easier to choose an airline.

Consider the similarity in the brokerage business. The great American tradition of expansion along chain-store lines has naturally affected the brokerage houses. Who am I to challenge the viability of chain-store operations in our wonderful world of Wall Street? Take Merrill Lynch, the largest of them all. I understand they hold some $20 billion worth of securities for their customers, a staggering figure. But in the opinion of this marketing and merchandising man, all large chain-store *brokerage* giants cannot provide the one ingredient that is the essence of all chain-store operations—the ability to save the customer money. Sears Roebuck is the classic example. With the best merchandising brains and cash resources, Sears can buy for less and sell for less, which they do. Their service is quite satisfactory in all departments, but they never claim to give more personal attention than the local specialty store. Chain stores could never grow in size and in importance unless they had a reason for being. The big attraction, of course, is that their prices are *lower.* Housewives—who, incidentally, make the decisions about where 85% of the family income is spent—all agree that they do the bulk of their shopping where the price is right, and that price is usually right below competition, particularly on branded merchandise.

Merrill Lynch—and I use ML only as a symbol for large, successful brokerage houses—deals only in "branded merchandise," the very same brands that are for sale throughout the land, and abroad too. I have often stopped by the Paris office of Merrill Lynch for the latest prices on Reuters' quotron. I must confess, they sounded better with a French accent. But at all times and places, as far as the *mechanics* of the investment business are concerned, one broker can execute your orders as well as any other broker and will receive the same commission for doing so.

Please note that I mention *mechanics* specifically. I am very well aware that executing an order is not the only function of a broker, but it *is* the only function where the payoff is consummated. And this payoff—the broker's commission—is price-fixed—irrespective of the amount of service or the quality of service that goes into executing the order.

I personally have graduated from buying ten or twenty shares at a time to buying a big block of a thousand shares at a time. I recently placed a large buy order for myself and for a client whose portfolio I manage. The commissions on those two orders amounted to about $600. I do my own research and make my own decisions. All my RR did was write out two orders; using the same amount of time, effort and thought he would on two small orders that would net the firm $10 in commissions. What is wrong with this picture? Perhaps, Socrates, the Great Adviser, can give us the answer.

chapter five

Socrates, the great adviser

Stripped of all semantics, the broker and the customer have one thing in common: they want to make a buck. In theory, the health of a brokerage firm depends on the health of its customers. In practice, the horizons are not so clearly defined. It is no secret that entirely too much stress is placed upon selling at point of sale. To be the big producer is the goal of every rep, and brokerage houses of high standing in the community openly and unabashedly advertise for "big producers"—that is, men accustomed to generating a large volume of commissions. It is evident that some monetary inducement is necessary to effect the change of employment. "We are salesmen," cry a great many reps. "If we don't produce, we had better find another means of feeding our families." The customer's health is never mentioned; the dollar sign looms larger than ever.

One of the things I've learned from studying Socrates is that a physician whose patients are all sick and feel worse than when they started his cure will not stay in business very long. And a brokerage firm that is losing money almost as fast as its customers will not fare any better, no matter how much it is allowed to raise the commission rate. Incidentally, while we're on the subject of doctors—(you will understand a bit later why I pose the following query)—when patients in failing health seek a new physician, are they apt to look for one who is reducing his fees?

It isn't necessary for us to compute the exact costs of running a brokerage house nor to determine what percentage of the total costs are charged to research and advisory personnel. Common sense tells us that in a bear market, when daily volume shrinks and prices per share also drop precipitously, the total take that reaches the till is doubly affected. Coupled with fixed research and communications costs, it doesn't take very long for brokerage house balance sheets to oxidize from jet black to blood red. To cut down on the costly research and communication or eliminate research entirely—as some have tried—is no solution. And neither is adding a surcharge or raising the commissions.

On the one hand, we have the crying need to keep the brokerage houses alive and well. On the other hand, we have a growing number of so-called discount houses that will execute your buy and sell orders and save you a substantial part of the commissions. As a former advertising man, I can foresee a free gift era: the more shares you buy or sell and the more times your investments are churned, not only will your "savings" on commissions mount, but you will also have your choice of an electric clock-radio, a toaster, or perhaps a free one-way trip to Hawaii.

It all seems preposterous, and if it were not so serious a matter, I could enjoy the laugh. It is pitiful to watch an industry that has grown fat and prosperous through the years start to open up chain-store branches as if they were McDonald's hamburger stands, only to discover that very lean times loom ahead. Putting the emphasis on *income* is, to my way of thinking, entirely wrong. Why not put the blame on the *service* the broker is supposed to perform? The plight of the broker has worsened for only one reason: The true function of a broker is almost a forgotten thing. Perhaps our national wealth has grown so rapidly and our communications systems so fast that we frail humans cannot cope with the situation. The public is as much to blame as the brokers for the extreme lack of service that plagues the industry.

A score of years ago, I heard of a company called Haloid. You will read more about it in the chapter, "The Xerox Story." I recall what transpired at the time of purchase. My broker was Spencer Trask & Co., and my registered representative was my late sister, Sarah Mitchell. Her paramount consideration was always for the best interests of the customer. What she did for me, she would do for all her customers. And, I believe, so would most other brokers.

I asked my sister to look into Haloid. It was an over-the-counter issue, and not too much information was available. After a week or so, I decided—with her approval—to buy 100 shares at $30 per share. The commission at the time was about $20 (hardly enough to pay for the phone calls). And that, dear reader, was not the end of the transaction; it was hard to get OTC quotes at the time, and I had to bother her—a bit too often, I'm afraid—to get quotes for me. It was part of the function of a broker, and no one complained.

Speaking of commissions, however, I cannot let this once-in-a-lifetime opportunity pass without repeating that because of my stupidity or stubbornness or come what may, I am sitting with a profit of over $3 million on that $3,000 investment. The $20 commission was surely insignificant. And suppose it was another stock and I made a profit of $1,000. Would it matter if my commissions were $30 instead of $20? On the other side of the fence, if I lose $1,000, does it make any difference if my commissions amount to $30 instead of $20?

This is my simple way of illustrating that the broker's most important function is to make some money for me. I am not impressed with size. If I fear for the safety of the company that holds my securities, I would have my bank act as custodian. I can see no fringe benefits to induce me to stay with a broker whose advice has not proven profitable.

The adviser, then, turns out to be the most important cog in the wheel—or the axle itself—without which the entire system of transporting money from one person to another comes to a halt.

Despite all his importance, the adviser—the research man, the technician who reads the charts and charts our itinerary, whoever he is—remains a man of mystery. Actually, from the customer's point of view he is the Invisible Man. We never see him. All we ever hear from our registered representative is, "Our research man says . . ." or "Our technician thinks . . ." or "They all like . . ." and so on. The rep never sees them either.

My old friend Socrates said very simply, "If you seek an adviser, make sure he is competent in doing what you want him to do." And he added, "In all professions, the inferior are numerous and good for nothing; and the superior are few and beyond all price." All of which makes a lot of sense to me. If my broker has a more successful adviser than competitors, I personally would prefer to pay my broker an extra fee for handling my account. However, this is not possible under today's commission-rate structure because the adviser's fee is included in the commission you pay. The average customer gives absolutely no consideration to (1) the part the adviser plays or (2) the amount he is paying the adviser for his services. As far as the customer is concerned, he pays nothing (extra) for this service, and if he is paying nothing for this service, subconsciously he feels that is precisely what the adviser's service is worth. There is an enormous disparity between what Socrates says—superior service is beyond all price— and today's prevailing opinion that it is worth nothing.

Aside from the confusion that exists regarding the value of the broker-adviser's services, I think we all have almost forgotten just what the B/A is supposed to do to earn his keep. (I am going to refer hereafter to the broker as the B/A, hoping to update his image to that of a graduate student in the art of making money for his clients.) Remember Socrates: "Is not making money one of the noble arts?" And is that not what the B/A is employed to do? Certainly, he is *not* worth $10 or $50 or $100 or a few thousand just to fill in a slip of paper with your account number, the code name of your stock, the number of shares, the price and then check carefully the *buy* or *sell* column, which happens to be *all* the service I get from my B/A. Admittedly, that's all the service I require from him, but surely many prospective investors need more service than that from their B/As.

In the old days, I did receive service worth far more than the commissions I paid, and so did everybody who asked for it. My broker spent oodles of time getting me reports on a company, advising me when to buy it, if that was the conclusions, executing the order and, then, for as long as I held the stock, keeping me advised of its action as well as of any special news in the economy generally or in my stock in particular. And when I got advice to take a profit or a loss, my broker had a mighty good reason for that decision. There was none of this hustling and churning, getting you to take a quick profit or a loss and switch into another stock—at least not with my old broker. That broker never grew fat on **my** commissions, I am sure. How come the firm is full of over-weight heavy-weights today?

Since we are all agreed that the adviser's contribution is the most important ingredient in a broker's service as far as the client is concerned, let us get the great man into our discourse. Socrates may be mostly remembered for having partaken of a hemlock cocktail, but little is known of his acumen as a business man. When needled by a friend who asked, "If you're so smart, why aren't you rich?" he cornered the market for olive oil and made a fortune. Which makes his advice to the investor who wants to become rich all the more pertinent. From some of his dialogues, I would like to quote some of his wisdom: In the Platonic dialogue called *Laches,* Socrates was asked for the best way to choose an adviser. He answered:

> When you call in an advisor, you should determine whether he is skilful in the accomplishment of the end which you have in view. Make him tell you that, Lysimachus, and do not let him off.

In the *Enthydemos* dialogue, said Socrates:

> Dear Crito, do you not know that in every profession the inferior sort are numerous and good for nothing, and the good are few and

beyond all price? . . . Are not gymnastic and rhetoric and money-making and the art of the general, noble arts? And do you not see that in each of these arts the many are ridiculous performers? . . . If you were engaged in war, in whose company would you rather take the risk—in company with a wise general, or with a foolish one?

In the *Meno* dialogue:

A mender of old shoes, or patcher up of clothes, who made the shoes or clothes worse than he received them, could not have remained 30 days undetected, and would very soon have starved.

It may pay you extra dividends to re-read what Socrates says and try to digest it thoroughly, word by word, in relation to your investment decisions. Most of us eat too fast, read too fast, and think half-fast. But harking back to my original premise, if there is such a wide gulf between the adviser who is good for nothing and the adviser who is beyond all price, how can we evaluate each? And, more to the point, how can we determine which is which, particularly when the costs of their services (extant or not) are included in fixed and identical brokerage commissions?

Let us suppose that you need major surgery and that there are several highly rated clinics or hospitals and that their fees are identical because they are fixed by a governmental agency. You cannot choose the surgeon who will perform the operation because you are channeled to him through an intern. (This situation is similar to your relationship to stock investing. Your customer's man chooses your B/A.) With your life depending on the success of the operation, which clinic would you choose? And with your financial well-being dependent on the successful operation of your investment portfolio, which broker would you choose?

There is no doubt that the present rate structure, which all brokerage houses must adhere to, will sooner or later have to be augmented, with a separate fee charged for the adviser or advisory department. To some extent, some brokerage houses have already instituted special charges for handling an account on a discretionary basis or under other special circumstances. In all cases, however, these charges are in addition to the regular commissions. One prominent brokerage house that specializes in institutional clients sells an elaborate advisory service to banks and institutions for some $10,000 a year. However, if the client generates enough compensating commissions, on a two-for-one basis, the annual fee is absorbed. This solution does not appear to be ideal because ill-advised wheeling, dealing, churning, and overtrading can easily creep into the picture. It is not good business for the broker or the customer to have any agreement that depends on the amount of commissions generated.

To my way of thinking, the simple solution is to separate the mechanics of the brokerage business, whose costs are certainly high enough and getting higher, from the research and advisory business. In a *New York Times* interview, Robert W. Trone, vice president in charge of Merrill Lynch, Pierce, Fenner & Smith's securities research division quotes some interesting statistics. "As the world's biggest stockbroker, Merrill Lynch also ranks as the top producer of pamphlets, industry reviews, economic forecasts and computer-fed stock ratings (2,416 individual issues are monitored constantly). . . . Each year, Merrill Lynch spends more than $6 million on research. The division itself encompasses 331 employees, including an even 100 analysts—at least twice as many as any other brokerage firm."

This gives the reader an inkling of the work and costs involved in operating the research department of the largest brokerage house in the country. And yet, how can we determine what this research is worth to the customer? I have a simple yardstick: it all depends on whether I am making a profit on my investments or taking a loss. If it is the latter—as is so often the case in prolonged bear markets, no matter how often the Merrill Lynch bullish bulls come stampeding into my living room on the television screen—I'm looking elsewhere, trying to find a better adviser.

Calling Athens, operator, long distance.

chapter six

Success is spelled
M-A-N-A-G-E-M-E-N-T

Years ago, the *Ladies Home Journal* promoted its advertising pages with the slogan, "Never underestimate the power of a woman." It paid off, and it furnishes me with an excellent theme: Never underestimate the value of management in its many applications, especially to the management of your securities—after they have been purchased.

If you think about it seriously, I am convinced you will realize that when it comes to your own investments, most of your own time and that of your broker's (if he is in the picture) is spent studying all the data you can assemble on one or two companies, watching their market action, making comparisons, and so on, then putting in your buy order. After that, what?

Has it ever occurred to you that the purchase of a stock is *not* all there is? That there's very much more to do to get on that road to riches? Apparently, your B/A has no further interest in the transaction; there is nothing in it for him. He's delighted, of course, if your stock goes up; even more delighted if you decide to take a quick profit and switch into something else. That makes two commissions for him where none existed if you leave it alone. I have come to one conclusion why so little attention is paid to managing one's stockholdings, individually and collectively. People simply do not understand what good management can do—in every business, in sports, and in our daily lives.

When you read my two chapters about Xerox, you will appreciate what I think of the value of management. We don't have to be reminded that bad management can ruin a successful company and good management has often taken a bankrupt company and put it on its feet again.

In everyday life, it's not surprising to see two wage earners in the same company, earning the same salaries, paying the same withholding taxes; one lives well and the other is always in debt. Management makes the difference.

Let's take the game of poker. I played a fairly good game as a youngster and gave it up—as a youngster—when I found myself playing on into the wee small hours of the night. We only played for a nickle or a dime, and I figured sleep was more important. Most losers think poker is a game of luck; it definitely is not. The consistent winner doesn't hold better cards; he simply manages to do better with them. The secret of winning lies in the way he manages his bets.

If management is the keynote to success in everything from five-card draw to the Xerox Corporation, you can guess how important it is to the proper care and feeding of your portfolio of stocks. And unfortunately, this is one aspect of the invest-

"Xerox"

ment business that is least understood and most under-estimated. For example, not everybody who buys a stock at a certain price on the same day *reacts* to its progress the same way. Even the jackpot winner of all time, my Xerox, did not blast off (as many believe) like an aerospace rocket heading for a rendezvous with Skylab. Actually, I held it for two years, alternating between a profit or a loss of several hundred dollars. Several of my friends got disgusted with its action and got out at a small profit or loss. One switched into another company that looked better; unfortunately, it broke him. Another needed some money to put down on a house, and who can blame him. These Xerox holders were just a few whom I knew personally; thousands of others had thousands of reasons for selling. All we know is that only a very few had the stupidity, the stubbornness, or the foresight to stick with Xerox—as I did—through thick and thin. And believe me, there were thin times, as in 1962, when it dropped almost in half from a high of 160. I had my reasons for persevering, of course, and they turned out to be right.

Buy + Hold

2 yrs. of Profit + Loss.

Thin Times, "Xerox" (cont)

Let us examine a portfolio of stocks that includes Xerox. While Xerox keeps going up in price, most of the others keep going lower and you get a call for more margin. Would you say that the one who held Xerox and took his losses proved to be a better manager than the one who sold all his Xerox and held his losers? And how much would you pay the better manager?

Let us add a few more parts to this question. Is this portfolio manager and your adviser one and the same man? If so, which part of him is more important? And is he being paid—for making you a richer man?

As far as I can tell, the answer to the $64,000—or

more—question is that there is no distinction between the adviser and the portfolio manager, and it really doesn't matter who is more important, because under our present system their services are *free;* it's all included in the one commission you pay. At least, their services are included in theory. It's really ridiculous to expect to get for free the kind of service I have found necessary to make money in the market instead of losing it. Here are a few things a competent portfolio manager must do *after* the purchase is made.

1. He must follow the daily gyrations of each stock in your portfolio.

2. He must follow the affairs of each of the companies in which you have a stake.

3. He must relate the progress of your portfolio to the economy and to other companies (not in your portfolio).

4. He must patch up your "old clothes," repair them, or replace them with a better looking inventory.

5. He must decide when to take a profit.

6. He must decide when to take a loss.

7. He must decide when to buy more on the way down.

8. He must know when to buy more on the way up.

9. He has to judge if it's time to switch—move to a different neighborhood.

10. He must know when it's justifiable to be bullish, bearish, or squeamish.

And here are a few more jobs for the portfolio manager:

11. He must keep abreast of any developments that might affect your holdings.

12. He must keep alert, able to spot another Xerox-to-be in the offing, even if it will take several years to mature.

13. He must also be able to pick the one new issue out of the dozens he looks into that will become the talk of the Street; and should it go sour, he must be able to get out with a big profit—at least 24 hours before it collapses.

14. He must keep the portfolio flexible and with enough buying power to take advantage of a special situation.

15. And, of course, he must always show a profit. (Just one little loss and off with his head.)

16. He must never be guilty of *missing* a stock that spurted 10 points 15 minutes before the close yesterday. (From a call the morning after: "How come you didn't get me in; surely your firm with its connections must have known about it.")

17. He must be brilliant enough to forecast a bullish turn-around when everybody is bearish and be astute enough to do this six months before it happens. Consequently, he must have an excellent track record for buying at the lows and selling at the highs.

I may be overlooking some trivia, like picking an occasional jack-pot winner that multiplies five or ten times in price in short order. But let's be realistic. Aren't these the skills you want your portfolio guided by? And doesn't it seem absurd that all the costs pertaining to these 17 acts of management—plus the even greater costs of channeling this expertise through to the one individual who is handling your account—should be included in the one commission, and at a rate that is fixed whether your broker has a large staff of analysts and advisers, a small staff, or none at all?

In my first book, *How to Make Big Money in the Stock Market,* I voiced the same opinions advising the readers that they would fare better with their investments if they had more respect for a customer's man's time and did not bother him daily to look into half a dozen stocks they had heard about. It may appear that I am fighting for higher fees for the brokerage houses. This is not so. The point is that there *is* money to be made by intelligent investing in the stock market, and the key to making that money is careful management of your investments. Skilful and attentive management is rare, and it will not become any more common so long as brokers are paid the same fixed rates whether they give good advice, bad advice, or no advice at all. I simply advocate a system of remuneration in this complex investment business in which the consumer pays a fair price for what he buys and the seller is paid for his labors.

I was literally pushed into the investment advisory business. A few readers who liked *How to Make Big Money in the Stock Market* came to me and asked me to handle their portfolios. They gave me full discretionary powers plus a check to cover my management fee for the first six months' service. They were complete strangers with $100,000 portfolios and they came to me unsolicited.

In mid-May 1970, I ran a few ads in *The New York Times* acquainting a waiting world of investors that I was ready to help them. My advertising prowess must have remained intact, even though I had retired from that business, for I was deluged with hundreds of inquiries from all over the country—many from account men in the largest brokerage houses.

I found that I had a great deal to learn of the behavior of investors, particularly with reference to advisers who put a price on their services. The time of the inquiries from prospective clients was, you will note, mid-May 1970, when the market was hitting new lows daily—after many of these prospective clients had, on average, lost more than half their money in 1969. The *fee* seemed to be the big stumbling block. One prospect lost $160,000 of his $300,000 worth at the beginning of 1969. "Your 2% fee is too high," he said. "Do you really believe 2% is too much to pay when unquestionably my management of your portfolio could have saved you from your $160,000 loss and perhaps turned it into a profit, just as I did for the clients I have?" I asked. There was no answer.

Another unhappy caller showed us how his $750,000 portfolio dropped to $186,000 net during the same period; to make matters worse, he was paying $25,000 a year in interest on his debit balance. "It's killing me," he added. Practically all he had left was 12,000 shares of a utility. My son (and only assistant) looked it up and found that the utility company had a huge debit balance that accounted (in our opinion) for the low price it was selling at. We recommended that he cut down his own debit balance and sell off some of his 12,000 shares. We also recommended that he switch some capital into a utility we knew and liked very much. (Incidentally, the stock we suggested has almost doubled in price since.) The poor chap was slowly going broke, but he completely ignored our advice.

I can remember having to tell a doctor who came to me and showed me one of the sickest portfolios I had ever seen that it was breathing its last. "If you could see your portfolio as I do, you would order an emergency heart transplant." He chose to continue the treatment he had been getting, and I am sure the patient died.

I soon realized that it is a very difficult task to educate the investor to pay for something he thinks he has been getting for free. I believe that you get what you pay for, and if all you are paying for is to have your representative put his pen to paper to write buy and sell orders, you aren't going to get very much. Some ink, some paper, and some action on the floor of the exchange, but nothing in the way of management. And a portfolio that doesn't get good and constant management is like a garden that doesn't get weeded—the weeds thrive, and they choke off all the flowers.

chapter seven

Las Vegas

Some members of the investment fraternity may take this author to task for daring to compare the antics of various Wall Street traders to those of the much publicized habitués of Las Vegas. It's ironic that many of these critics casually admit that they do "play" the market on occasion but refuse to believe that there is any resemblance to gambling in their market activities. I do not for a moment question their sincerity; all I hope to do is point out the many similarities between playing the market and Las Vegas. Henny Youngman knows the quickest way to beat Las Vegas: When you get off the plane, walk into the propeller.

Participants in both games have one thing in common: the urge to make a fast buck, to hit the jackpot, to find another Xerox, to get rich overnight or, rather, before the night is over. Unknowingly, they have another thing in common: instead of coming up roses, they come up losers every time.

Another similarity is the absurd nonchalance of many supposedly sophisticated investors who buy a stock with as little forethought as they drop a quarter into a one-armed bandit or toss a colored chip onto the roulette table. This is not an exaggeration on my part; I have often pointed out that many buy-or-sell decisions are made in less time than it takes to select a $3 necktie.

Another similarity between Wall Street roulette and Las Vegas roulette is the emotional factor, which is far more obvious at the roulette table than it is in Wall Street but far more costly to the players on the Street. It is rather sad to see the crowds of men and women at the roulette table, dropping their chips wherever they may fall, switching them around at the last second before the tiny steel ball starts its orbit. And its an equally sorry sight to watch investors choose stocks with the same emotional hunches they use to pick roulette numbers, switching and changing up to the last minute, and hoping against hope "that Lady Luck is with them on their investment bets.

One advantage the roulette player has is that he can enjoy instant losses, whereas the Wall Street gamesman must wait for months, even years, watching what he affectionately calls "paper losses." I have known men of great wisdom (in their own businesses) who are thoroughly convinced that paper losses don't really matter because the Internal Revenue Service does not recognize them as deductible until the stocks are sold. However, as I mentioned to an argumentative friend, *banks* recognize paper losses. They will never lend you a penny on them, but banks are eager to lend me money on my paper *profits*.

Let us leave the roulette table and take a few steps to the dice table, which appears to be even more active at two in the morning. I gather from the happy participants that this game's popularity stems at least partly from the beautiful cocktail waitresses who generously proffer drinks to the players without charge. Or is it the fact that here too losses are instantaneous? There is a certain thrill to be found in the very act of losing a great sum of money with a swish of a drink in the presence of beautiful women. Recall Cyrano de Bergerac throwing the purse that contained his month's wages to his admiring followers. When his aide cries, "Think of what you have done," Cyrano replies, "But think of the gesture!"

Perhaps there is a bit of Cyrano in most of us, which might account for the following incident pertaining to how some people buy stocks. At a gathering a short time ago, a friend and I were present when a certain stock was discussed. A few of the big shots concluded it was a hot stock. Their broker was also present. "Buy 1,000 for me," one ordered. "Pick up 500 for me," said a second trader, "And pick up 500 for me too," said a third. My friend joined in, "Buy 300 for me." That was the total extent of the "group analysis" of the stock in question. I think I have hit upon a new definition for the term *group analysis* that may explain (in my opinion) so many sure-fire instant losses.

Back at the dice table, I once saw a really spectacular incident that I should like to tell you about. The time was nearing 3:00 A.M. when a statuesque young lady wrapped in a lustrous dark mink coat walked over to the table and asked if she could roll the dice once for $3,000. For such a sum of money, the croupier had to call one of the managers to okay the bet. One glance at the coat, and the manager agreed.

The croupier rolled the dice to her and as she picked them up, she casually dropped the mink coat off her shoulders to the floor, revealing her naked entirety. If it had been the fourth century B.C. and Praxiteles had been there, he would have immortalized her in marble as Venus at the Dice Table, so perfect were her proportions.

The Las Vegas Venus rolled the dice just once, leaned sensuously across the table, picked up her winnings, re-wrapped the mink around her shoulders and swayed grace-fully out of the room, the eyes of all still focused on her.

The first one to break the silence that ensued was the manager. He glanced at the croupier for the first time since he sanctioned the bet and asked: "What was her point?" The croupier quite honestly stammered: "I didn't see it either."

Neither did a single one of the habitués standing close by see her point, though they witnessed the whole proceeding most attentively. And who can blame them for forgetting the game at hand when confronted with a distraction of far greater interest.

It may come as a surprise to learn that Wall Street traders are faced with somewhat similar distractions almost daily. I am not implying that the distractions on the Street are as revealing as those of our Las Vegas dice thrower. Actually, *full disclosure* (which the S.E.C. requires in every prospectus) would save many an eager buyer from making a fool of himself by getting out of a good stock to get into an unproven, new, hot issue.

Almost daily, in one form or another, a seemingly glamour

stock enters the scene; perhaps it is even provocatively wrapped in mink. And the various stock holdings that we have become accustomed to are all but forgotten. Could it be that the switching urge to make a fast profit is as great as the sex urge, or even greater? What else can explain why a mass of buyers will suddenly stampede to a new glamour stock that just came to town? No one thinks of looking at credentials. No one stops to think that all that glistens is not glamour. No one questions why the stock has tripled in price overnight. No one, that is, except those who remained faithful to their old dividend-paying favorites.

You might think that one great stock disaster would be enough to cure us of our ills. But, as the wit says, sex is here to stay and so is the urge to switch. There is little hope left ever to regain the *profits* lost or to put our house in order unless we learn a lesson from the past—from the drop-outs who once were high-riding, high P/E favorites but now have dropped out of favor, dropping up to 90% of their value on the way.

Emerson wrote one of the most famous heroic couplets in the English language:

> . . . if eyes were made for seeing,
> Then beauty is its own excuse for being.

To which I must add my own not-so-heroic couplet:

> If stocks are part of your being,
> Look twice at what you think you're seeing.

And in the bitter cold light of reality, ask yourself this pertinent question if you ever fell for any of the attractive drop-outs: What was your point in buying them? An honest answer, I am sure, would be: I didn't see it either.

chapter eight

The truth about Mr. Tips

A century ago in London an unknown diner gave a small gratuity to a waiter *to* *in*sure *p*romptness, which explains the origin of the word *tip* and a nefarious practice that persists to this day. In our wonderful world of Wall Street, an equally nefarious practice was started by an unknown investor who probably bribed some clerk to secure inside information about a company before he bought the stock— *to* *in*sure a *p*rofit. After that, tips abounded everywhere—for a fee and for free. In some instances the tipster was paid to pass on specific tips to manipulate an unsuspecting public that was, unfortunately, all too eager to make a dishonest profit.

Before researching Mister Tips more thoroughly, I would like to remind my readers that I have a phobia about losses. I dread them like the plague. I simply hate losing money. I hope my phobia rubs off on you. Please note carefully that many of these chapters are designed to help you avoid losses in the stock market. I don't want you to give our wonderful world of Wall Street a bad name. Until you learn the truth about Mr. Tips, you will be doing great harm to our image as well as to your purse.

Mister Tips is really a conglomerate composed of touts, imposters, and parrots—a motley group if I ever saw one but, withal, a very impressive one. The big problem is to learn how to distinguish between the trusted and the tout, the real and the imposter and, most difficult of all, one parrot from another. The truth is, not all parrots are bad birds, but which ones should you listen to?

When Sol Linowitz retired as Chairman of the Board of Xerox in May 1966, Joe Wilson had just paid high tribute to him by saying, "They never made an important decision without Sol." Sol replied, "Reminds me of the time they crossed a parrot with a tiger. I don't know what they got, but when it spoke, you listened!"

Wouldn't it be wonderful if we could find such a half-breed to tell us what stock to buy and—we might as well dream on—when to take a profit? We might be able to improve our batting average if we learn to separate the touts, the imposters, and the pauper parrots from the professional parrots— research men and analysts—and the improsario parrots— with a record of successful performance behind them. There are plenty of parrots around worth listening to, and they shouldn't be hard to find. Some 12,500 are members of the Financial Analysts Federation, a national organization of various local societies of security analysts. The largest group is the New York Society of Security Analysts, which has a membership of about 5,000. About 2,500 have passed a series of examinations and have earned the Federation's designation of <u>Chartered Financial Analyst.</u> Nothing is *sure,* but at least these pros have had some training and should know what it's all about. According to C. Reed Parker, C.F.A., and past president of the *Financial Analysts* Federation in its *Journal* (September/October, 1970):

> The concept of professionalism for the financial analyst is far more precise than once it was. The body of knowledge requisite to skilled performance of our jobs is now quite well defined. And it is a broad body of knowledge. It is a blending of the disciplines of economics, accounting and statistics into the specialized framework of security analysis and portfolio management. We have created programs that stress and encourage our acquisition of the knowledge and the constant refreshment thereof. These programs include the Financial Analysts Seminar now held on the Rockford College campus each summer, the Canadian Investment Seminar held on the University of Western Ontario campus and the Investment Management Workshop at Harvard.

No one can deny this highly sophisticated group of financial analysts their right to be named to the Order of Truly Important Parrots. To keep "constantly refreshed," in addition to their daily jobs they regularly attend daily, weekly, and monthly meetings, luncheons, dinners, and seminars at which high-echelon representatives of companies of great interest to the investment world present the latest developments in their respective enterprises. Progress, new product development, research, earnings, and so on are outlined. After these presentations, the meeting is thrown open for questions and answers. Each analyst is thus able to keep his own valuation of these companies' stocks up to date. When these parrots talk, it is worth listening to them.

Of lesser stature, I list some semiprofessional customer's men and women—50,000 60,000 in number—all of whom have passed certain examinations required by the New York Stock Exchange to be designated as registered representatives. Many of them are analysts as well, and I am sure they would all agree that they deserve the truly important parrot title. They are the immediate, and usually the only, contact the investor has with his broker. They are, of course, very gregarious. They do a great deal of talking, relaying the opinions of the higher-ups to their customers. Lack of time, the avalanche of questions and quotations concerning countless stocks, the impatience of investors to get in immediately on every situation that strikes popular fancy, all these factors make it necessary for the RR—a lone human being after all—to resort to the mimetic powers of the parrot. More often than not, the average RR is reduced to repeating what he has heard without fully understanding what he is saying.

It is at this point that the parrot's undesirable qualities begin to assert themselves, and it can happen whether the market is booming or busting. In a bull market, for example, increasing gains registered on the Dow seems to trigger optimistic chatter from broker-parrots. Individual stocks score big percentage increases daily, and impatient investors scramble to get on the bandwagon. Unheard of (unrealistic is too mild a word) P/E ratios are paid for new issues that have not stood the test of time. The customer's man is overworked. Brokers are beseiged with new accounts. Offices are added or expanded, all to the drone of the parrots in the background. You can't really blame them. They scarcely have time to think, and the song they sing never grows tiresome. "Stock prices are going up! ABC is going to hit a hundred, *two* hundred, who knows?"

In a bear market, the tone may be different, but the parrots are forced to chatter nonetheless. "I got the information from a good source." "Who knew that the Dow was going to drop to 600?" "It's the banks' fault. They're charging me 12 percent." Volume declines, and brokers start complaining that they're losing money. Branch offices close and customer's men are dropped to the drone of the pessimistic parrots in the background.

I don't want to be too hard on RRs. It is understandable that they haven't the time or the desire to fight the worst qualities of parrothood. Why think very hard about what you say when the financial reward is going to be the same whether your advice is good or bad? But I do intend to warn you, the investor, that your RR is going to parrot, and you would do well to be very cautious about listening to his chatter—and, more importantly, acting on it—until you are convinced that what he is saying comes from a pure-bred Truly Important Parrot.

There are 4,000 or more advisers and advisory services who receive a fee to manage investors' portfolios. We must, of course, include them in the professional TIP ranks. The market letter writers, of course, cannot be rightfully called parrots, since their's is the printed word, but I suggest approaching their *written* chatter with the same wary skepticism I've advised you to use whenever you approach an unproven tipster.

The total number of Wall Street parrots represent a sizable slice of the population of the United States. Their influence on our daily lives is inestimable. This is evidenced by the amount of chatter you hear daily about financial happenings at every stratum of our modern society. Parrot patter about the ups and downs of Wall Street is, perhaps, the nation's greatest preoccupation. I can think of no other pastime that can count so many devotees. Talk, however, is cheap (except on the telephone, long distance), and when it comes from the parrots of Wall Street, we must evaluate not only the parrot but what the parrot is saying.

To attempt to total the number of pseudoprofessional parrots is an impossible task. Their numbers are exceedingly large, for 'suspects' can be found among the following:

Thirty-three million stockholders.

Everyone who works for a broker, an analyst, an adviser, or a corporation listed on the New York or American Stock Exchanges or issues a leading over-the-counter stock.

Husbands and wives of investors, as well as their in-laws.

And I must include a fast-disappearing breed of men who for generations have had the unique right to barge into the private offices of many of the richest and most important men in the financial community—genial, gregarious shoeshine boys.

Neither the extent of the pseudoprofessional parrots' numbers nor the importance of their influence on the buying, holding, and selling of securities can be estimated with any degree of accuracy, but by their own talk—which certainly resembles the mimetic powers of our feathered friends—we have to believe that they are far more influential than they deserve to be.

Mankind could not survive on this planet if our fine feathered friends did not control the population explosion in the insect world by devouring several times the weight of their bodies in insects every day. This is nature's scheme of things. The bird population is also controlled in some fashion. A friend of mine, a city-bred homeowner in a small community in New Jersey once had a beautiful cherry tree on his property. One evening, as he put his car in the garage, he encountered a black snake. And like all us cityfolk, he clubbed it to death. A neighbor nearby, hearing the commotion, came over to see what was going on. When he saw the dead snake, he told my friend that he might as well cut down his cherry tree. He explained that snakes are very fond of raiding the catbird nests often found in cherry trees to eat the catbird eggs, thus controlling the population explosion of the catbirds. Sure enough, it took only one season for the catbirds to hatch in great numbers and devastate the red ripe berries they hunger for.

Whereas the birds in nature do their good deeds for us by keeping the insect population in check, I am not so sure that the parrots of Wall Street have as obvious a beneficial effect on the financial community. With all due apologies to the professional segment of our parrot population—and as a member of that particular group, I intend to assume the right to judge—I should like to clarify my criticism by evaluating their services. Only then can we better understand how they affect our finances and our daily doings.

Unlike nature's way of preventing population explosions, we have yet to discover a way to stop the Wall Street parrot population explosion. I have repeatedly observed that once an investor makes a profit on a stock he bought, forever after he claims the right to be a parrot—to give advice to others. And he exercises this right freely, despite the fact that he has been wrong on every other stock transaction he ever made. He will argue with you quite logically that all his losses resulted from advice he received from other parrots—the dumber ones, as contrasted with his own category. It should be noted here that a dumb parrot is not necessarily speechless.

Because I cannot even *estimate* the total number of parrots that brighten or darken our financial skies nor deliniate the infinite variety of the species, I categorize them all as Mister Tips, for that seems to be their ultimate function. As a further amplification, I would like to introduce a new category—the pigeons—which defines those who listen to and follow the advice of the parrot willy-nilly, thereby validating the oft-heard expression, "You're a dead pigeon."

Success in Wall Street—and that means having your money make more money than it could lying in a savings bank—really narrows down to a battle of the parrots and the pigeons and on which side you deploy your assets. To a greater cr less extent, we are all dependent on Mister Tips. Our successes or failures in the stock market, however, are determined by our ability to separate the parrots from the pigeons. It is not easy when you consider that a forlorn pigeon may be masquerading as a prosperous parrot.

Anyone who has a long record of making money in the stock market has learned how to distinguish the real from the fake and the phony—by instinct, experience, and thorough investigation. I think you will find it worth your while to read what I say about the different parrots I have met through the years. I know them all and understand their parrotese (parrot talk) very well, and that accounts substantially for my own success in making a fortune for myself. I therefore urge you to follow my parrot studies carefully and they will help you to stop losing, and start making, some real money. The parrots are not all to blame; share the blame yourself if you're always looking for a hot tip. I have a new slogan to replace "Stop, look, and listen." It is "Listen, and stop looking."

To help you recognize the many parrots that cross your way and, perhaps, to learn to understand them, I will describe a few of them.

The Ideal Parrot

Of a retiring nature and is never seen in crowds. He is seldom seen or heard. His basic philosophy appears to be, "Those who know don't talk; those who talk don't know." But when he does give an opinion or an evaluation about a certain security, you may rest assured that what he says is based upon reliable information—very, very reliable. Yet, his experience and his record of successful investments notwithstanding, he makes no positive promises of what the market will do today, next week, or in the months that lie ahead—because he simply does not know. He can give you an accurate picture of a company, its products, its management, its research, and its profit potential. If you get to know him well, he may even give you an indication of when he thinks you should buy the stock in question.

The Informed Parrot
The Intelligent Parrot
The Inquiring Parrot

These TIPs all wear the same plumage as the ideal parrot and command your attention and consideration when they talk. Be sure their information comes from a reliable source. I strongly lean toward the inquiring kind, who ask many questions to enable them to analyze a company in depth and gather the intelligence necessary to come up with the right answers. Whether their advice proves to be right on the nose on every stock they recommend is not of real importance at the moment. There is never a sure thing. But I prefer to put my money on this kind of studied advice rather than gamble on the advice of the ill-qualified parrot, whose guessing average is heavily weighted on the losing side.

Far more numerous than the ideal, the informed, the inquiring parrots, are—

The Ill-Advised Parrot
The Ignorant Parrot
The Imperfect Parrot
The Incompetent Parrot
The Imprudent Parrot

It is difficult if not impossible to distinguish one parrot from another by plumage or by the sounds they make. Yet, there are differences, although they are not easily discernable to the naked eye. Herein lies the secret that separates the boys from the men, the successful from the perpetual losers. To the unsophisticated, it appears that the successful investor is possessed of some mystical power that not only guides him in selecting the best of the glamours but also keeps him away from trouble on all the rest.

The five aforementioned parrots all sound alike. In fact, their tips may sound even more impressive than those better qualified. My advice to my readers, therefore, is to be wary of all parrots unless you are sure their advice is not going to net you a loss.

And if you are genuinely interested in avoiding losses in the stock market, do what this Papa Parrot has always done. Whenever anyone gives you some advice on the market, whether or not you are sure what kind of parrot he is, ask him the following questions:

1. Where did you get the tip? What is the source of your information?
2. Have you made any money lately?

3. What happened to that hot tip you gave me yesterday (or last week, last month, or a year ago)?
4. How come your wife is wearing last year's pearls?

And don't *buy* unless these questions are answered to your satisfaction. And *never buy* because some of your fine-feathered friends are buying too.

And *last* but certainly the *most important* TIP to remember is that the great bulk of Wall Street Parrots have one thing in common with Mother Nature's most beautifully plumaged Parrots: They may *mimic* the human voice, but they don't know what they are talking about.

chapter nine

The Khans of Wall Street

From my discussion of parrots, you must realize that I am interested in exotic birds. Some of the most exotic characters throughout history have been the Khans, and it may come as no surprise to you that these figures are related to our wonderful world of Wall Street. A Khan is really a ruler or leader in Mohammedan countries. The Khans I am most concerned about at the moment are Genghis Khan, the Aga Khan, and the Khans of Wall Street—a rather incongruous group of characters.

The Khan most widely known is Genghis Khan, the first of the great Khans. He was the Supreme Ruler of the Moguls in the 12th century. Hordes of his barbaric warriors swept through the Asian and Turkish nations, ruthlessly slaughtering those who tried to resist them. What intrigues me is some of Genghis Khan's methods; today, we would call them psychological and fifth-column tactics. At times, these conquering hordes would send their emissaries ahead with sweetly phrased messages, professing to come in friendship to promote prosperous trade between the nations. At other times, they would send fifth-columnists among the peoples they wished to subdue, spreading tales of their barbaric invincibility. Those were savage times; the envoys often returned without their heads and their beards, both of which were considered grave insults that had to be avenged with even greater slaughter. The end result was the same—annihilation—whether the invaded peoples resisted or were "khanned" into submission. Eight centuries later, these tactics still exist, only we have changed the spelling to "conned."

In the 19th century, the British, great colonizers that they were, rewarded the incumbent Aga Khan by making him a semi-independent ruler over some 50 or a 100 million Indians. The Aga Khan was worshipped as the spiritual head of all Ismaili Muslems, not only in India but throughout the Moslem world.

His millions of subjects were faithful and generous, and had a quaint custom for showing their devotion: On each birthday, the Aga Khan was given a gift—his weight in gold or precious gems. So as not to become monotonous, one year it was diamonds, another year it was sapphires, another year, emeralds, another, rubies, and so on. Incidentally, he was one of the heaviest rulers of our time. Another quaint subsidiary right was that the water he bathed in was bottled and sold at a good profit. (The water was considered to be holy and of therapeutic value.)

Some enterprising young underwriters missed an opportunity to have the late Aga Khan go public. With AK earnings growth dependent on population growth, which is relatively high in India, the stock would rate a high price/earnings ratio. And, important to the investor, the risk on the downside (birth control) is neglegible. Some of today's hot issues are about as sensible!

The third notable Khan, the go-go Khan, is not a relative of the Aga Khan, nor is he a Moslem, but he has a strange hold on an undisclosed percentage of the 33 million shareholders in the United States. His influence is tantamount to that of a spiritual leader, but its effect has proven far from beneficent on the investment world. The affluent go-go Khans have accumulated their great wealth at the expense of their loyal followers in the financial community. Khan is, of course, an assumed name—rather a euphemistic and shortened version of con man—which accurately describes the nature of these potentates. The name can be applied to individuals occasionally, but more often it is appropriate for certain well-organized syndicates. Highly paid attorneys keep the Khans' operations just within the law. Occasionally, a prominent Khan slips up, is exposed, fined or jailed, or flees to foreign shores to avoid further prosecution. Nevertheless, despite adverse publicity, the go-go Khans are so skillful in infiltrating the best of society, so persuasive in their operations, that even after the individual investor has suffered a substantial loss, his faith in the basic tenets of this speculative sect persists, even though his belief in a particular Supreme Khan may have been shaken. This is a phenomenon that exists only in a certain speculative segment of our financial world. In other fields, con men seldom swindle the same victim twice. In the stock market, however, once a man is bitten by a Midas bug that promises to double his money overnight, the speculative fever cannot be controlled. His portfolio may shrink with one loss after another, but rarely can he tear himself away from the prospect of a quick killing.

It is difficult to distinguish go-go Khans from the legitimate brokerage houses, customers' men, research analysts, and advisers. Their true identities are very well hidden, and their aides may be among your closest friends and associates, who innocently and unknowingly spread their propaganda. The most dangerous go-go Khan is the one who admits his identity to you and for some reason or other (which will escape you at the time) decides to take you into his confidence. You sort of become his bosom pal and ostensibly are allowed (or taken) into a sure-fire deal he is cooking up. It could be a new issue or one of the listed stocks. What makes it all sound sincere is that the Khan readily admits that what he is doing just skirts the law, but with the skilful manipulations of his organization, all hands will get out very close to the top—just when the sucker public starts getting in. And since you have suddenly become a "partner," you stand to make a very handsome profit. Smokey would warn you to stay away from your new bosom buddy—as far away as you can travel, to another state if convenient—because he may turn out to be a dangerous pyromaniac.

If any of my readers choose to ignore Smokey's warnings or do not appreciate Smokey's ability to sniff the scent of a distant smoke-screen long before it becomes visible to the human eye, let me add some words of wisdom from a guru who personally related to me an interview he had with a Supreme Khan. He was surprised to hear the Khan say, "You cannot con an honest man." He went on to say, however, that few men are completely honest and devoid of larcenous tendencies. The skillful Khan man can detect the slightest trace of larceny in his intended victim, and that is all he needs to sense for him to make his pitch. He relates how his group made a million and a half on a previous deal and says regretfully, "Too bad I didn't know you at the time." The hook is baited, and next time the Khan comes around, all too many suckers grab the bait and don't feel the hook until it's too late. I have seen some very respected and canny businessmen fall for this go-go line. Invariably, after a few months, my snookered friends come back to me and say, "Those go-go Khans turned out to be crooks, but I switched to a new group. They're smart boys, all of them. They sure know the ropes."

The surest way to avoid losses is to be wary of anyone who speaks like a con man and of innocent parrots who make sounds like a con man but don't understand what they are talking about. I can spot them a mile away. When one of them tells me, in strict confidence, that his group are the ones that pushed ZYX from 20¢ to over $20 a share, I run a mile in ten flat, which is an extraordinary feat for a grandfather who hung up his sneakers many years ago. The same is true when he tells me, "They are buying it 5,000 shares at a time." I know darn well nobody in his right mind will tip me off to buy a stock before he has his. Nor will anybody who owns a block of stock that he is ready to dump tip me off to get out before he unloads.

Be wary of Khan men; better still, pass them by completely. Remember, nobody has been given his weight in gold since Aga Khan III died, and the chances are extremely poor that the practice will be revived with you as the recipient.

chapter ten

The devil's seven disciples

We all know what God was doing for the six days of
Creation, but no one seems to know how the Devil was
kept occupied at the time. I contend that the Devil was then
at his busiest, calling together his seven most devilish disciples and instructing them how to disrupt and destroy the best
laid plans of those who would dwell in the land of Paradise
(renamed Wall Street at a much later date).

There is ample evidence that the Devil's seven disciples
are actively engaged to this day in the investment world,
surreptitiously driving unsuspecting investors down the road
to ruin. Who they are, how they work, and the incalculable
damage they do is the subject of this chapter. Be forewarned,
I will name names and promise full disclosure.

The Devil's number one disciple is the Egomaniac. What
makes him so dangerous is his ability to assume various

disguises; he sneaks up on you unaware and is most difficult to recognize because he is often indistinguishable from *your own ego.* Do you want mathematical proof of the damage the Egomaniac has inflicted *on you* in particular? You can have it if you dare be honest with yourself. Usually it is easier to recognize this demon in others.

To listen to the countless conversations in Wall Street boardrooms, at the club, on the commuter's special, the Madison Avenue bus, the subway, or the Chock Full O'Nuts lunch counter, no one is ever wrong. It's always the other fellow's fault—a clear indication that the Egomaniac is in full control. Do you recognize this plaintive wail? "I could have made a fortune in XYZ but 'they' put me in RST and I lost my shirt."

It is ironic that failures adroitly tune out their mistakes while successful men delight in telling about their biggest ones. The late Billy Rose repeatedly told about a young lady he auditioned in Dallas who was told by him that she would never make it on the stage; she turned out to be Mary Martin. Note how the amateur ego shields his errors of judgment and talks only about the time he sold a stock right at the top, right before it collapsed; or the one time he got an eagle on the 460 yard 17th (though he's never birdied it since).

Study a group of veteran investors; give them all the same facts, figures, and projections relating to one specific recommendation. Of course, they will all react differently. But if you continue the study in depth, you will be amazed at the variety of questionable decisions made because of man's inability to control his ego. For example, a friend took a profit on a stock; a few weeks later, the stock moved up—which is not a calamity; he had taken a substantial profit. I asked him a routine question: "Why did you sell?" His first reply:

"My customers' man was bearish and urged me to sell." I knew this was not the truth; it was denied by the c.m. He hedged with a few other reasons like, "I needed the money," "I want to put some of my money in tax-exempts," and so on, all of which are good and sufficient reasons. Then why not say so in the first place? Since the stock had gone up, the seller found it necessary to *appease* his ego. Would his reply have been apologetic if the stock had gone way down, instead of up? Appeasing your ego or giving it undeserved credit doesn't increase your ability to take the best course of action in the market. On the contrary, you are slowly but surely losing confidence in your ego; you cannot continue to fool yourself.

The second-in-command of the Devil's seven disciples is named Itch-Witch, a most vacillating companion. Posing as the friendly angel of good fortune, she is welcomed into the most respectable portfolios. Pretending to enrich you momentarily, she possesses an amazing power that may impoverish you.

There is no doubt that everyone loves a profit, and the Itch-Witch is seemingly the best friend an investor ever had. But this is far from the truth. I have encountered many happy investors who, after succumbing to her profit mania, wound up broke. Contrary to general expectations, this happens more often that we care to admit. Let us examine how the witch works. One of her most popular slogans is, "You cannot get poor taking profits." This bit of wisdom was initially attributed to Baron Rothschild, whose financial acumen is well documented. It is repeated daily by thousands of friends and well-wishers—at the witch's wishing well. Frankly, most people need very little urging to take a profit.

Ironically, "taking a profit" can be, and frequently is, the most disastrous bit of advice one can follow. This apparent contradiction and confusion stems from a four-letter word that completely changes our motivation. The word is *itch*. Compare the following:

1. To take a profit!
2. The *itch* to take a profit.

It is important that you learn to distinguish one from the other. You may have many good and sufficient reasons to "take a profit," but I cannot name one worthwhile enough to satisfy the prevalent *"itch* to take a profit." This itch has ruined more investors than any other human frailty. There is an obvious explanation why this is so. The timing cannot possibly be right, since the profit is taken without regard to the stock itself.

Moreover, once you are in the power of the Itch-Witch each profit increases your itch to do it again. And here is where she is at her destructive worst. You are now at her mercy. The profit has stimulated your ego. You have no time to think clearly. Forgotten are your good intentions to evaluate a stock intelligently *before* you buy or sell it. Now all you are itching for is another quick profit. Your next hunch may result in a loss, a very big one, but that's only a temporary setback (the Itch-Witch assures you), and you are now more determined than ever to satisfy that itch. I have observed many once-healthy portfolios waste away to oblivion.

The entire subject of profit-taking has, in my opinion, received less consideration than any other factor in planning an investment program—from financial writers, analysts, advisers, and investors themselves. Why this is so is one of the anomalies of the investment world. In reality, it should be the *best understood* factor. Is it not the one determining factor that measures the extent of your success?

Study a few of the reasons that motivate the investor to take a profit. They are not listed in the order of their propriety or importance.

1. You need the money.
2. You fear that the market in general is due to decline.
3. The future of the company does not look promising.
4. The outlook for the industry is bearish.
5. You fear your profit will turn into a loss.
6. You believe that you will be able to buy the stock back at a lower price.
7. You want to buy another stock you believe will do better.
8. You have a tax loss; therefore, you can avoid paying any tax on your profit.
9. You have taken so many losses, you need a profit to bolster your ego.
10. Your wife's brother thinks you should sell.

You may have a few reasons of your own to add to this list, but please note *particularly* that (with the exception of 5, 8, and 9, which obviously refer to profits only) these same reasons apply *equally* well to taking a *loss*. The point I stress is that whereas losses seem to be a forbidden topic of discussion, the moment you have a profit, the pressure starts and keeps mounting as your profits rise: "Take your profit," "Take half," "It's not a profit until you take it," "You can't get poor taking profits," and "You'll be sorry." I counsel you, do *not* let the Itch-Witch stampede you into taking a profit unless you have an honest reason for doing so.

The Divorcee, the only other female member of the Devil's disciples, is known for her coquettish beauty and her born prerogative to change her mind—as well as yours. Her trick is to activate the switch game: For one reason or another, many of us indulge in the Divorcee's favorite pastime—switching from one stock to another, hoping to improve our lot. We need no special persuasion. The Devil's Divorcee has no particular interest in the normal, contented investor who is happily married to his portfolio. Her natural prey is the fellow with the roving eye, never content with his profits, forever seeking greener pastures and happier mating grounds. To do her justice, I must confess there have been times when these daring rovers actually hit the jackpot. In the long run, however, you will fare better by avoiding her, though to do so may seem rather tame. Let us examine her less harmful tactics.

A stockholder buys 100 shares of AXB at $20, and some months later, it is selling at $30; he has $1,000 profit. He is getting itchy when he meets one of the Divorcee's friends, the appealing issue RST, which is also selling at $30, and she appears far more interesting. So he sells AXB and brings RST into his love nest.

Meantime, another stockholder who some months before bought RST at $20 and, like our first fickle friend now has $1,000 profit, in like manner meets AXB, gets excited about her, and switches his RST into AXB.

What have they both accomplished? Aside from the novelty of watching their new friends "perform," they each have lost two commissions and the tax on their profits. These harmless flirtations are costly, and that's the best you can say for them.

All switches are not so harmless. Some can be disastrous and break up a happy home. Let me cite one with which I am very familiar. This one was actually recommended by a reputable broker among a score or more tax loss switches. It was made after Xerox dropped to 125 and a fraction. "Switch Xerox into Texas Instruments." (The price of the latter was a bit lower than XRX.) In about a half-year, Xerox hit a new high of $313, as compared to Texas Instruments' high of 144¾. I don't know of any other switch with such a disastrous result. For the sake of the broker who recommended it, I hope his other switches fared better.

There are, of course, switches that make sense. I would recommend a few. For example, you own a stock in an industry that is dying; whether you have a profit or a loss, it makes good sense to switch into a stock in a live industry. You own some Chrysler and it is your understanding that Ford is increasing its share of the Big Three sales volume, at the expense of Chrysler; Switch Chrysler into Ford—or vice versa if the figures change. On one occasion, I owned over 150 Xerox debentures convertible into 150 shares of Xerox common stock. Since the debentures were selling at a premium of about $36, I sold the debentures and switched into 200 shares of Xerox. I made a profit of 50 additional shares that I wouldn't own if I waited until the debentures were called. There are countless others that can deliver a profit when you can accurately evaluate the potential of each end of the switch.

One word of caution: Do not let the alluring Divorcee charm you into any of the following switches no matter how exciting they look. Beware the quickie switch, the summer romance: Your intentions are not very honorable; you knowingly sell your steady, dependable stock to buy the exciting newcomer; you are sure you will have some fun (make a good quick profit) for a few days, then return to your "steady." It doesn't work out that way; you are more apt to become involved in a long engagement, hoping to make up your loss. And to sadden you further, the "steady" you discarded has become a high-flying glamour stock pursued by countless suitors. This bit of poetic justice is not a figment of my imagination. My script embraces hundreds of actual stock transactions I personally witnessed—and I seriously hope relating them in this fashion will have a deeper impact on your stock evaluations than if I were to repeat some daily laments you hear repeated and repeated and repeated. They usually follow this pattern: "I got a hot tip on Triple-tronics; it has to hit 100, maybe 200; so I sold the XYZ I've owned for years. Now I'm stuck with Triple-tronics. If I ever get even, I'll be happy." Does it sound familiar?

Here is another switch to avoid! Beware: "Why don't you sell 100 shares of Xerox and switch into 1,000 shares of UVW? If UVW goes up a point, you make $1,000. Xerox has to go up ten points to equal that." Or, "Switch your 100 shares of MNO at $20 into PQR selling for $2. You can get 1,000 shares; if it only goes up to $4, you will double your money." Don't waste your time even considering them. The opposite is more apt to occur. Some while back I tried to advise a fellow tapewatcher. Studebaker was selling at $7, and Xerox was selling at $140. I suggested that he get out of 200 shares of Studebaker (which he was holding for years at a loss) and switch into my favorite. "What can I get," he asked, "only ten shares." I asked him, "Do you think your $1,400 is any larger than my $1,400? It only looks larger to you because you're thinking in terms of 200 shares." Of course, he stayed with his Studebaker. Ironically, Xerox split five for one whereas Studebaker had a reverse split, one for five.

Then we have another type of switch. Slowly through the years the conservative investor has built a successful dividend-oriented portfolio; he has followed his plan to buy sound income stocks and bonds for his retirement. At this point he may be introduced to some attractive opportunities to switch into some action stocks and make some quick money. I strongly advise this investor never to risk any part of his retirement money. He has played it safe up until now; this is no time to get aroused by the Divorcee's smiles.

Yet another switch is far more dangerous than is apparent on the surface. This concerns the "big shot" success, the envy of his friends. He has amassed very substantial profits in *one* glamour stock. He can afford a flirtation with the Divorcee, or so he thinks. With her devilish assistant, the Egomaniac, it is easy to feed the big shot's ego. He enjoys hearing her whisper, "With your know-how, you can double your fortune. Why hold on to your slow-moving stocks? Get rid of them and double up on your glamour stock." This switch may succeed for a short while, but the day of truth is sure to arrive. One fine day when you are a bit overextended, the market collapses—and so does your portfolio. You will note the break always comes when you least expect it—just before you planned to get out. But *no one* is that smart.

In conclusion, I do not wish to leave the reader with the impression that I am particularly antagonistic to the Divorcee. In truth, she has never been unkind to my portfolio. My only advice to a prospective two-timer is think *twice*—you will have to—for you have two problems: You must evaluate *both* ends of the switch and be *right both times* to wind up a big money winner. It's not notoriety you are after, it's making money.

It is often very difficult to determine which of the Devil's disciples is the most destructive, the Egomaniac, the Itch-Witch, or the Divorcee. At times all three gang up on you. They work so smoothly together, you may not be able to distinguish one from the other—particularly when you have lost a great deal of money. I have observed, notwithstanding, that the Egomaniac is the greatest culprit. This may be difficult to document (in a court of law) because *you*, yourself, may be the Egomaniac and will refuse to testify on the grounds that it may incriminate you. Of course, you may blame the one who told you to take your profit; you may also blame the one who switched you into a very substantial loss. You may think you are appeasing your own ego, but that will *not* retrieve your fortune. A friend of mine, a man of means, told me he had taken a few thousand dollars profit but his *losses* (on his new stock) were staggering. "You cannot make money that way," I replied, as I reminded him of the dialogue between two famous vaudeville comics, which went something like this:

> "What have you been doing lately?"
> "I've bin in the horse business."
> "What's the horse business anyway?"
> "Well, we buy horses and pay fifty dollars apiece for them. Then we feed them for six months and that costs us another fifty dollars. Then we sell them for seventy dollars apiece."
> "You can't make money that way."
> "Yeah, we found that out."

Yeah, you cannot make money that way in Wall Street either. But perhaps reading about these losses can teach you how to *avoid* them in your own transactions. If you can learn this important lesson, you will be on the road to prosperity. You may contend that the only sure way of avoiding losses is to put your money in a sock, but even that can be lost or stolen.

Among the Devil's seven disciples, there are some lesser lights. In this complex investment world, one must learn to recognize them. One of them is named the Avenger. Somewhat shy and seemingly distant, you will find him warmhearted and most sympathetic. He has a penchant for appearing on the scene when you are seeking consolation most. You will welcome his friendship and find it genuine and longlasting. You may wonder why he is called the Avenger, which begets the image of the stone-faced cowboy who spends years tracking down the culprit who shot his best friend in theback. Is this the same man who has been called "the best friend a loser ever had"? It is, and you will soon learn why.

In sharp contrast to the good-fellow-well-met—the fairweather friend who helps finish your bourbon while toasting the killing you made in the market—the Avenger appears when the stock you recently acquired starts declining. Your ego is happy to hear him assure you you'll get even in a few days. The stock may go down a bit more, but the Avenger (he is now your buddy) proclaims he'll never let his buddy take a loss. (How often have you heard a friend say, "I am not selling until I'm *even?*") It amazes me how prevalent this get-even determination is. It is difficult to break up this devilish friendship after it reaches the buddy stage. Even when the loser is forced to sell and take his loss, the Avenger assures him, "I'll get it back for you," and he really tries. And he will keep trying time and time again; he has plenty of time—your time. Many investors hold onto a stock at a loss for ten or more years. Then, one day, with a triumphant gleam in their eyes they declare, "I got *even* today. I sold my XYZ." What is this mysterious power that casts this senseless spell upon your senses? Is your ego so strong that you fear to offend it? Are you not completely overlooking the countless opportunities you missed through those years? Think back! How many times could you have bought another stock and more than doubled your money—enough to make you forget the trivial loss you were carrying on your books?

In a similar situation, I discussed the Avenger with a fellow tapewatcher, without mentioning him (the disciple) by name; I prefer to keep out of the Devil's way. My friend had just bought some American Photocopy at $13 a share. Having had some experience evaluating this stock, I commented that I was still bearish and asked him what made him bullish. This was his motivation: "I lost a lot of money on this stock and hope I can get even." I chided him that this was no reason to buy a stock and continued, "I am sure if you look around you can find a better opportunity to make up your loss on APY." I suspect, however, if you were capable of questioning his ego you would find he actually would get more satisfaction out of making $500 on his APY than making $1,000 on another stock.

Human frailties being what they are, I urge my readers not to treat the Avenger too harshly; at times he may be helpful. It is difficult to end that kind of a long-lasting friendship abruptly. The best you can do is accept him for what he is and, by all means, don't forever keep heaping all the blame on him. After all, he wasn't responsible for your loss in the first place, or have you forgotten?

The next disciple of the Devil you are likely to meet is the Explorer. You will find him fascinating—a handsome adventurer forever on the move, searching the far corners of the world for the most glamorous girl of his dreams, a buxom blonde called Miss Fortune. (Please be careful when you spell or pronounce her name.)

The Explorer lures the investor of above-average intelligence who happens to be sitting with a pretty good profit. But being overly active or imaginative (which aren't bad traits at all), he becomes discontented (impatient) with his profit and sets out to conquer a stock entirely foreign to him. And all this while, right at his elbow, he overlooks a number of good stocks he can buy with a greater degree of safety and perhaps a greater potential.

Notwithstanding, the Explorer does have some redeeming qualities that have won him many friends. He is never lazy; you can depend on him whenever there is work to be done. He believes good fortune does not come to those who sit idly by hoping a bonanza will fall into their laps. He knows enough to go looking for it. His obsession with the uncharted and his love of adventure may carry him into areas where angels fear to tread. On the other hand, he dislikes crowds, particularly unruly crowds, who emotionally and unerringly make the wrong decisions. (Many stock analysts today have adopted the odd-lot theory, which reasons that when the mass of small odd-lot traders are buying, it's a good time to sell, and vice versa.)

If you are looking for a devilish good time and can afford the *risk,* the Explorer always has room for another passenger. He simply loves company (but then, so does Misery).

From the Explorer, we move on to the Wood Carver. You may indeed wonder how a humble wood carver could ever attract the attention of the Devil and become one of his disciples, particularly in view of the fact that we first learn of him as an apprentice wood carver in the little north Italian town of Assisi, which is best remembered for its religious pageantry. The students vie with each other, as well as with the master craftsman of the day, to have one of their gracefully sculptured madonnas carried in the parade on some festive occasion.

At an early age, the Wood Carver had so distinguished himself with his incomparable skill that he soon attracted the attention of the renowned Renaissance painters, who commissioned him to create gilded frames worthy of their great works of art. And it is said that many of the Wood Carver's creations were executed with such consummate skill that the art connoisseurs who beheld them often extolled the beauty of the frame far above the masterpieces themselves. It is recorded, much to the annoyance of some very celebrated painters, that the frames themselves often fetched a higher price than the paintings they embellished.

Posing as patrons of the arts, some unscrupulous dealers who were no doubt aides of some of the Devil's disciples, offered the Wood Carver great inducements to create gilded frames for them. Thus, paintings of very poor quality enriched with one of the Wood Carver's masterpieces fetched a very high price in the marketplace. On more than one occasion, the paintings themselves were proven to be valueless copies. (It is interesting to note that the word *frame* to this day has a criminal connotation.)

Such extraordinary talents of enhancing the value of a product were most certain to attract attention in some areas of the investment world. And you can readily understand how many a worthless security has been foisted upon an unsuspecting public, which all the more emphasizes my premise that you must diligently evaluate a stock before you buy it. Do not allow the glitter of the frame to blind you into over-paying for some obscure "forgeries" in the financial balance sheet of some high P/E securities.

Do not dismiss the Wood Carver and adjudge his influence on your buy-and-sell decisions too lightly. It is, of course, far easier to blame someone else for every loss you take; it is far wiser to learn more about the devilish influences that beset you, knowingly or unknowingly. It may help you to better understand the Wood Carver's activities, alone or in association with his culpable companions, by relating him to the Impatient Stone Cutter.

Though mentioned here as the seventh in line, the stone Cutter is a not insignificant member of the seven disciples. Ostensibly, he is a builder with a solid objectivity—which should be of great interest to every Wall Street investor. But he embraces a great many characteristics attributed to his six companions that collectively can and actually do ruin some of the best planned portfolios of stocks I ever reviewed. Again, I ask the reader to follow with interest what may aptly be called "The Rise and Fall of the Impatient Stone Cutter."

We first discover our engenue, an impatient youth, the son of a stone cutter in a remote village in ancient China. We find him sitting at the foot of a mountain, diligently chiseling away at a large piece of marble, tap after tap, bit by bit, until it breaks loose from the whole. This he finally shapes into a beautiful statuette with a skill comparable to the Wood Carver's. He then carted it to the richest man in the village and sold it to him for his garden.

At his side walked a genie—though invisible, I am convinced he was genuine. He told the Stone Cutter an incredible story of how he was imprisoned for ages in this very piece of marble and how he unknowingly freed him; he owes his life to him and in return promises to obey him. "Your every *thought* will be my command," he whispered. The Stone Cutter paid scant attention to the genie, delivered his statue, and returned home.

To the poor Stone Cutter, the rich man's home looked like a mansion and he thought, I should have a home like this. The genie obeyed and our poor Stone Cutter became a man of means. But his new-found happiness was brief. He was invited to visit the governor of the province who lived in a beautiful palace, had a large staff of servants, and several tiny palaces for his concubines. And he thought, if only I could be the governor. The genie complied.

And in like manner, our Stone Cutter became the Emperor of all China with grander palaces, wives, concubines. Now he was the most important power in all the land. But behold! The floods came and ravaged the lands, destroying homes and crops alike; darkness and famine swept the land and the Emperor was helpless. Surely (he thought) the Flood God was most powerful—so he became the God of the Floods.

But the Sun God appeared, brightening the land and drying up the waters and with its life-giving rays produced bountiful crops and the populace rejoiced. The Sun God must be more powerful than the God of the Floods (he thought)—and thus he became the Sun God, more powerful than the God of the Floods, more powerful than the all-powerful Emperor. Now he was supremely happy. Nothing could dim his smiling image (he thought) as he watched his all powerful rays reflected on the mountainside. Reflecting a bit further (he thought) the mountain stands proudly erect; neither the power of the floods nor the heat of the sun could move the mountain; hence, the Mountain God was the most powerful.

There in his lofty abode lived the Mountain God, content at last, a bit exhausted perhaps from his impatient travels, but supremely content—until his rude awakening. One day he heard a tiny tapping at the foot of the mountain. Tap after tap, day by day, the lowly Stone Cutter was breaking up the mountain. Bit by bit, the mountain was doomed to destruction. And the Mountain God thought, "What the Gods of the Floods and the Sun could not budge is being destroyed by a lowly stone cutter. Surely the stone cutter is the *most powerful.*"

The wise investor can learn a powerful lesson from the experience of the Impatient Stone Cutter—for it very closely parallels the stock manipulations of many who should know better. But let us first look into a very devilish scheme he cooked up with the aid of the Wood Carver. I believe the Egomaniac, the Itch-Witch, the Divorcee, the Avenger, and the Explorer all had a hand in it. Pooling their varied talents, they designed and built probably the largest and certainly the most ornate merry-go-round the investment world has ever seen—and they called it the Wall Street Carousel.

Of the 33 or more millions of shareholders in the United States, there are but a few who have been able to view the

Carousel in its entirety—to appreciate its usefulness to the investment world and fully understand its many pitfalls. There is no admission charge for an innocent ride on the Wall Street Carousel; in fact most investors do not realize they are whirling around on this carousel. The organ music plays on, perhaps lulling you into a false sense of security, or on occasion jolting your nerves with some rock-and-roll or go-go tunes.

In all seriousness, I urge the reader who is out to make a million in Wall Street to be constantly *aware of what he is doing.* When you buy a stock, you automatically become a rider on the Carousel. You may not think so, but you're there.

Rule 1: Select a comfortable horse. You may be in for a long ride.

Rule 2: Carousel horses keep moving up and down, so do not become over-elated on the upswings or panic on the downs.

Rule 3: Don't let the attractive Divorcee on a fiery Arabian stallion beguile you into switching horses midstream for a stock that promises more action but doesn't guarantee which way the action will go.

Rule 4: If you are enjoying your ride, don't let the Itch-Witch sabotage your portfolio of stocks with recurrent doubts and fears.

Rule 5: If you are not enjoying the ride and have a loss, change your horse. Don't let the Avenger talk you into getting even or you will be in for a longer ride than you imagine.

Rule 6: Remember, the Wood Carver's frames are all beautiful; examine the *contents* carefully. Bargains may prove to be counterfeits.

Rule 7: Recall in detail the progress of the impatient Stone

Cutter. Constantly hopping from one horse to another in the hopes of enriching your portfolio at every move may bring you right back on your Carousel to where you started—no richer, perhaps no poorer, and in most instances, no wiser!

And don't ever forget that you may be taken for a ride.

chapter eleven

The Wall Street Zoo

In addition to the extremely interesting Devil's disciples who roam Wall Street, there are some absorbing four-footed creatures native to the financial district you really ought to know about, particularly since some inhabitants of the Wall Street Zoo have habits worth emulating. And others, to be sure, have habits you must avoid at all costs—or you are sure to suffer some very painful costs! Not all the members of the animal kingdom of Wall Street are as well known as the bulls and the bears. As a studious research analyst, I thought it wise to explore their habits and habitats to better understand their effect on our investments. All you animal lovers are urged to come along, if only for the excitement.

How the bull became a symbol of ever-mounting prices of stocks, I do not know. The dictionary merely states that the bull is an uncastrated male member of the bovine family. Let us not forget that in size, he does not measure up favorably with the bull elephant or the bull whale. Perhaps the Street should hold these massive stand-ins ready for future use when the averages hit unprecedented new highs. Another exciting image of the bull is to be found in the bull ring where, ironically, his popularity is short-lived. Could this be cautioning our most bullish investors that even in the midst of plenty, the grim reaper may appear when least expected?

Bears, the foreboding symbol of disaster, have massive bodies, short limbs, and very short tails. They are able to stand up, walk, and dance like a man. They are dangerous, omnivorous, and very fond of honey. They hibernate during the winter months, losing much of the fat they accumulated during a bullish summer. The Wall Street term *bearish* may therefore allude to a bear's ability to smell out and raid a well-filled beehive and rob it of its honey. Or perhaps it is a subtle warning to unwary speculators that after hibernation, the bear, lean and hungry, may descend upon their well-stocked larders without warning and strip it *bare.*

The childhood story of the tortoise and the hare, brought up to date, reveals the conflict of two investors. The tough-skinned tortoise buys a sound, slow-moving stock; the flighty hare chooses a fast-mover. In one quick jump, the hare is halfway to its target. In no apparent rush, he rests on the roadside, dreaming of the romantic excursions he will soon take with his profits. The tortoise cautiously plodding along, soon overtakes his rival and wins the race. Many stocks, as you probably have already noted, follow a similar pattern.

The wolf is a carnivorous, rapacious quadruped with a mean, ravenous nature. A number of years ago, in Alaska, their population was sharply reduced by professional hunters. The health authorities pointed out, however, that there was a resultant great danger of a tuberculosis epidemic striking the natives. It seems the wolf packs hunting down the caribou (who were able to outrun the wolves), attacked and destroyed the sickly and tubercular caribou who lagged behind. Decimating the wolves meant the survival of the sickly caribou, which eventually would reach the dining table, infecting all those who ate the tainted meat. So the wolves were let alone and nature continued its own system of purification.

The wolves of Wall Street who populated the speculative areas and operated in packs (they are also called pools) so rapaciously in the 1920s bear a striking similarity to their quadruped cousins. They, too, attacked the sickly—those who try to get by on the thinnest of margins are their natural prey. Every investor who seeks to keep the wolf away from his door would be wise to eliminate any sick members in his portfolio. (I assume the portfolio has a solid brick foundation and the frustrated wolf can huff and puff till he's blue in the face but your stocks will remain intact.)

The lamb is a symbol of innocence and naiveté and is easily sheared of its precious wool. Nature has not endowed him with too much intelligence. It is said that a lamb, though close to a food supply, can starve to death because he lacks the initiative to find it. The innocent investor, however, though sheared of his precious wool, should have the intelligence to move on to more palatable pastures.

Contrary to his royal image, the lion-hearted king of the jungle is not the undisputed master of his lair. Travelers in Africa have often noted that even though the lazy lion has found a cool shady spot for his daily siesta, and is awkwardly but comfortably adjusted, his lioness comes along and snarls at her husband in a very domineering manner. The king immediately takes to his heels, vacating the coveted resting place for her highness. Perhaps the lion can subtly caution us that we may not be as important as we think we are. Even though we just made a handsome profit, we cannot rest on our laurels. (The lady may not like it.)

The giraffe is the tallest of animals, reaching a height of 18 feet 7 inches; though its tongue measures 18 inches, it is almost entirely voiceless. He can run as fast as 30 miles per hour. He has an awkward, knock-kneed stance as he stoops to drink at the waterhole, but it is one time, contrary to the laws of physics, that water runs uphill.

The ostrich is the largest of birds, weighs 300 pounds and is eight feet tall. Several hens combine to lay their eggs in one nest; the male sits on them at night, not so much to incubate them as to protect them from other beasts. It is said the ostrich buries his head in the sand at the approach of danger, but this may just be playing possum, for I am told that pound for pound, he is the most powerful antagonist in the animal kingdom.

Nature has endowed both the giraffe and the ostrich with long, powerful necks to facilitate their search for food; both are swift afoot, with legs so powerful, they strike terror in the hearts of their adversaries. Even the king of the jungle knows better than to attempt to attack a giraffe singlehandedly. The lionhearted investor who sticks his neck out and overextends himself to reach for a stock at an unrealistic price has no such assurance of survival when danger approaches. The wise investor might also emulate the male ostrich who sits on his nesteggs to protect them from disaster.

The mule and the ox are beasts of burden. The mule—with no pride in ancestry nor hope for posterity—though popularly

referred to as stubborn, is actually a very patient and sure-
footed animal. The ruminant ox chews his cud and patiently
mulls things over. Their relevance to investors is, ironically,
the opposite of what you might think at first glance. They
represent the kind of stocks that are the workhorses of Wall
Street; lacking surface glamour, they always pull their own
weight, patiently but with untold underlying vigor. You will
do well to include some of these stocks in your portfolio. After
all, work never killed anybody.

The tiger and the jaguar are both breathtaking felines, lithe
and graceful. But, like all felines, they are sly, stealthy,
ferocious, and treacherous. Even nature has abetted their
cunning, camouflaging their stripes and spots so subtly that
their presence is hardly discernible in their native habitats—
which is highly disconcerting to the unwary hunter who may
get too close for comfort. As an amateur painter, I fully
appreciate the beauty and color of the scene, but as an investor, I view the tiger and jaguar type of stocks exciting specula-
tions for the lionhearted as well as for the foolhardy. If that
is your cup of tea, be sure you have the stomach for it. It's
most difficult to judge which way these cats may jump.

The Arabian camel, or dromedary, has one hump and is
larger than the Bactrian camel of Central Asia, which has two
humps. They are both ruminant beasts of burden, and since
they are able to store water in their bodies and humps, they
can travel several days without refueling.

The fox, somewhat smaller than his courageous cousin the
wolf, has erect ears, a bushy tail, and a far more cunning
disposition. The patient, deliberate camel and the fox form
a rather crafty, though incongruous, pair of Wall Street traders; the fox with his acute sense of hearing may find an

attractive speculation that weathers the camel's approval because of its "hidden reserves." And together they can fare
well, provided, however, that the camel can keep his partner
from outfoxing himself.

The eagle is a large diurnal bird of prey of the falcon family
and is noted for its size, strength, powerful flight, and keenness of vision. It is the national bird of the United States and
appears on its gold coins. It may be significant that these
"golden eagles" being in such limited supply are now worth
several times their face value. Thus, the eagle-eyed investor
should be able to swoop down and catch on to a stock that
will make a lot of money for him, provided, of course, his
keenness of vision also encompasses a talent for envisioning
the future.

The dinosaurs that roamed the earth in the Mesozoic Age,
a mere hundred million years ago, were the largest known
mammals, but it is said their small heads and brains were
completely disproportionate—which may account for their
extinction, for they never possessed the knowledge to adjust
themselves to climatic changes.

In contrast, the lowly ant, whose remains were recently
discovered fossilized in rock formations estimated to be 100
million years old, is still with us in great numbers. These
hymenopterous insects live in communities, have an extremely high rate of intelligence and are notable for their
industry and organizational abilities. They have not only survived the vicissitudes of time but actually threaten the exis-
tence of mankind, if man does not learn to control them.

Here we have an example of the lowly ant thriving millions
of years after the demise of the formidable dinosaur—a far
greater contrast in size than David and Goliath or Jack and

the beanstalk giant. I like to be reminded periodically (as I look into the potential of some small companies) not to underestimate the power of management—when it is comparable to the all-talented, albeit lowly, ant.

The reader may have noticed as he wanders through the Wall Street Zoo that there does not seem to be any compound available to house the popular primates. This is not an arbitrary omission on the part of the author. I am informed by the keeper that real estate values in this small island area are extremely high and it would be economically prohibitive to rent a space large enough to comfortably accommodate all of us primates (or speculators) who would qualify for admittance—as inmates, of course.

chapter twelve

The subject is asses
(or how to save your own)

have allotted a separate chapter to one inhabitant of the
Wall Street Zoo because he follows a practice—currently
in vogue, it seems—that is potentially disastrous. I am talking
about the ASS, a participant in the growing group of Amateur
Short Sellers. I cannot, of course, indict *out of hand* the
process of going short. This technique certainly has its place
in the financial community, but I insist its place is not at the
whim of an amateur, whose battle cry seems to go:

> Ashes to ashes, dust to dust,
> If all the bulls are going bust,
> Can I do worse selling them short?

Over a century ago—a period that some called the Era of
Frenzied Finance—some of the events on Wall Street were
fantastic. Financial titans of the day fought each other to gain

control of a company. Corporations were formed, went public, merged, bought, sold, bankrupted, re-formed at bankrupt prices, and resold to the public at unbelievable profits. At the same time, opposing groups, or "pools," as they were called, often "sold"—that is, went short. And the spoils went to the strongest group. None of the rules and regulations that govern short selling today existed at the time. In the old days, stocks could be dumped (short) at any price, thus precipitating further declines.

If I remember Wall Street history correctly, Commodore Vanderbilt, the great railroad magnate who practically owned the New York Central Railroad, received a charter from the Council of the City of New York to build an elevated railroad along Third Avenue that was to be the rapid transit system for the growing population. A corporation was formed, and its stock was naturally in high demand. Meantime, a group of men that included some powerful city officials conspired to sell the stock short, have one of their men in power revoke the charter, and cover their short positions after the stock collapsed, as they were sure it would. The charter was revoked—but the price of the stock kept rising. The Commodore kept buying every share offered. He knew that he already had more shares than were issued. He had cornered the stock. And in those days, he could demand that the seller deliver the stock to him and pay him any price he asked for it. The popular refrain of the day was:

> He who sells what isn't his'n
> Must buy it back or go to prison.

I don't think any of the conspirators was jailed, but they were all impoverished by the Commodore's just demands.

I do not wish to infer that because this or other short transactions come to grief, short-selling is without merit. But I do wish to say that in the hands of an amateur who sells short, on a pure gamble that the price of the stock will drop further, is a dangerous, and sometimes ridiculous practice. I have always said, gamblers don't gamble, especially if the odds are only even.

If I were contemplating going short, I certainly would not be satisfied with an even break. The risks are much higher when you are short. When you buy a $10 stock, all you can lose is that $10, but if you are short a $10 stock, there is no telling how high the price may be when you have to cover. I would, therefore, study the situation *more* carefully than when I buy a stock; and you know by now how I advocate giving thought. Also, I would not concentrate on just one security to go short; I would study a few others, too. And if I found one whose earnings are slipping and whose future potential is deteriorating, and I have reason to believe they are going to lay off a great many workers, and the president may resign under pressure—and these facts are not generally known—I would conclude I had a better than even chance to make a profit by going short.

For more sophisticated, tax-minded investors and traders, there are certain tax advantages to practices such as selling short against the box. Personally, I am not that sophisticated and stick to my old-fashioned belief that tax considerations should not unduly influence the decision about when to sell a stock. I have observed too many investors who want to get out of stock that they consider too high in price hesitate because of what they will have to pay the government; such hesitations are often lengthy in duration and very costly.

There are many good reasons for going short, and if you are intrigued with the idea, consult a professional when such situations come to your attention. A simple arbitrage opportunity may exist when mergers or takeovers take place or are about to take place. For example, stock A and B are going to merge share for share. A is selling for $25 and B is selling for $22. If you go short by selling A and you buy B, you cannot go wrong, unless the merger is called off. Just a word of caution; remember, the news is out. You are not the only one who knows about it. If the disparity in the prices of the two stocks persists, others with more money than you have are not sure the merger will go through.

The asses that concern me most, and they include many odd-lotters, are the amateur short sellers (whose initials I have corralled) who believe they have found a new investment strategy that will, in the natural course of events, retrieve their losses and net them a profit. Their reasoning is *short* and simple: "I could have sold XYZ at its high; I honestly had it in mind at the time but I was too busy to act on my own advice. That was six months ago and I could have had a 30 point profit. But the market looks worse now than it did then. I cannot sell any of my stocks; my losses are too big. So I will sell XYZ short now; it should go down another ten points." Doesn't this all sound familiar?

The foregoing is a single example of the crimes that are perpetrated daily in our wonderful world of Wall Street. Yet, the crimes and the culprits are hardly ever apprehended. Sherlock Holmes would have instantly spotted the clues, the crimes, and the culprits. And I can see Perry Mason in a dramatic court room scene ask some of these questions:

Q: Did you ever sell short before?

A: No.

Q: Why did you pick XZY?

A: I wanted to make a quick profit.

Q: Did you have any other reason?

A: Yes, it had dropped faster than any other stock on the Big Board.

(Objection, your Honor. The witness is trying to impress the jury by using the term "Big Board" as an indication that he knows what he is doing.)

Q: Didn't you look around to find another stock to sell short, one that might drop faster than XYZ?

A: No, it never occurred to me; I only wanted to make 10 points, $1,000. I am not too greedy.

In the summation, it was shown that many crimes were committed by this amateur short seller. Primarily, he knew nothing about company XYZ, its product, management, earnings, and potential growth, as compared to its competitors. Nor did he make an effort to get some tangible information about the company. He never considered the price/earnings multiple of XYZ or compared it with the P/E of some stocks he held in his own portfolio. All he did know is what some parrot told him: "You can make money going short as easy as being long." He did not know that the parrot did not know what he was talking about, either. And another ass was born.

The jury, naturally, will be sympathetic to the culprit, for they too have had similar experiences, which they blame on the bear market. However, justice will prevail. The laws of the land categorize these crimes as self-inflicted, and more often than not, the punishment is inevitable as soon as the crime is discovered. Consider yourself forewarned: If you go short naively—without investigating the kinds of companies you should concentrate on, the past, present, and future status of these companies, and the best timing for your move— you'll gain nothing more than charter membership in the Royal Order of Unmitigated Asses. And the only reward to be garnered from that distinction is a loss, and lots of company. . . . The kind of company you must avoid.

chapter thirteen

The Xerox story

You may have noticed that the name "Xerox" has crept into this narrative from time to time, and you've probably guessed that my attitude toward Xerox is definitely positive. In fact, your reaction probably sounds something like this: "If I had made $3 million on one company's stock, my attitude toward that company would be positive too!" Well, I'd like to tell you the Xerox story, not to crow, but because there are two valuable lessons to be learned from it, both aspects of the same characteristic—*management.* I want to point out some of the things you should look for in the management of companies whose stock it will profit you to own. In addition, I will tell you how I managed my Xerox investment from the day I first became interested in the stock up to the present.

This five-letter word, Xerox, the registered trademark of the Xerox Corporation, has become a symbol of incredible success, especially to the Wall Street community. The mere whisper along the street that "this may be another Xerox" is often enough to send a stock skyrocketing. It was not always thus. Let's travel back some 20-odd years to record the actual circumstances that preceded my purchase of Xerox.

To begin with, there was no Xerox at that time. There was a company in Rochester, New York, called Haloid. Its founder came out of Eastman Kodak (which was good recommendation for him, in my opinion). The company itself manufactured a line of photosensitized paper, much of it used for photostats. As an ad man, I knew all about stats. Haloid did about $15 million a year in business. I heard that they were working on a process of some sort that was sensational; if they ever perfected it, the stock would really go places. So, I began to check around.

Actually, I could find out very little about the process or the progress they were making. In fact, the little I did glean was that their progress was plagued with disappointments. My photostat makers told me it was a good company, nice people to work with. My broker confirmed what I had heard, that a large company put some Haloid away for its old-age pension fund and one or two knowledgeable investors put some away in their portfolios. I considered this information bullish. Haloid was selling over the counter in the low $30s, and I decided to put $3,000 away for the Mitchell old-age pension fund.

The initial market action of Haloid was not very promising; the over-the-counter bids fluctuated from the mid-20s to the upper 30s; earnings were basically static for a few years. Two of my lodge brothers (who, incidentally, owned Haloid before

I got in) decided to get out with a small profit and advised me to do the same. One of them cautioned me: "They have a hundred competitors doing the same thing." My investigation told me a far more bullish story. I visited Rochester and talked to some Haloid men. I came away with the feeling that this new "xerographic" process was not to be compared with other copying machines on the market. It was worthwhile gambling on Haloid's future, and I continued to hold the stock.

After a few years, progress must have continued, because the price of the stock (evidently reflecting this progress) reached the $100 mark; it was not a spirited rise; along the line I recall times when it was difficult to get a decent bid for Haloid. One can get very discouraged with an over-the-counter stock when bids grow scarce, even at lower levels. Moreover, I was now sitting with a profit of some $7,000, which isn't bad for a $3,000 investment; and even my best friends kept telling me, "You cannot get poor taking profits." Rather than worry about my profits, I kept getting more interested in xerography, trying to learn something about its application to industry. My philosophy about over-the-counter prices was contrary to that of my friends and associates. As its price went higher, I became more bullish. For example, I would learn through some of my very reliable sources and sometimes through public announcements that Lehman Bros. or some other important institution was buying Haloid in volume (at a price two or three times the price I paid). Common sense told me that since Haloid was paying such a small dividend and already was selling at a high price/earnings ratio, the only reason they could have for buying blocks of Haloid was that they knew something about what was coming.

Now is no time, I concluded, to get off the bandwagon when so many important investors were busy climbing aboard.

Around 1955, the stock sold above $100 and split three for one. I now owned three hundred shares of Haloid. The company put on a show at the Waldorf Astoria to introduce Copyflo. The performance of Copyflo completely fascinated me and, I believe, everyone who witnessed it. From a microfilm nested in an aperture card, Copyflo produced one to fifteen copies blown up to 24 by 36 inches (two by three feet sounds even larger) at the rate of six a minute, all automatically, with the turn of a dial (for quantity) and the press of a button—on an ordinary sheet of paper, dry and smudge-proof—and as clear as the original blueprint, down to the smallest four-point type.

I learned further that the storage, retrieval, and reproduction of blueprints posed very costly problems for large manufacturers. Huge warehouses were needed to house them; hours and days were consumed in locating them. Meantime, highest paid engineering staffs lost even more valuable hours and days awaiting them. The Haloid Xerox Copyflo was the solution, a revolutionary time- and money-saving device. Punched aperture cards could be filed in five percent of the space the originals would require, thereby reducing warehouse rental costs by 95 percent. The wanted blueprints could be almost instantly retrieved and reproduced. The value of the labor hours saved was incalculable. If my memory serves me right, by using Copyflo, Westinghouse saved some $400,-000 in labor costs alone in one year.

It was during this Copyrama that I had the pleasure of meeting Mr. Joseph C. Wilson, the President of Haloid Xerox (Xerox having been added to its name). I introduced myself to him as one of the fortunate stockholders who got into the stock a number of years before and had stayed with it. "You're the kind I like," he commented. I found him most cordial and easy to talk to, and I got the feeling he was prone to understate things.

As I continue with my analysis of Haloid Xerox, I want to remind you that all the foregoing events took place over 15 years ago but my thinking then was no different than it is today in relation to the motivation for buying, holding, or selling a stock. You will note that even then when so little was known about Haloid, I paid scant attention to whether I had a profit or a loss (a policy that I still pursue today, with all my stocks); rather, I concentrate on the company's performance and its management.

From time to time, being an advertising idea man, I would become excited about some plan and a letter went out to Mr. Wilson. One suggested that publishers of magazines with multimillion subscribers could put 1,200 names on a single microfilm aperture card and, with the speed of the Xerox Copyflo, print 480,000 labels in an hour. Mr. Wilson replied that this plan was not flexible enough for the publishers, but my letters were always warmly received and Mr. Wilson never failed to thank me for my interest in Haloid Xerox.

At one time, I seriously considered going into the service end of Xerox. The Copyflo rented for some $3,000 per month, which I figured was too much for a great many companies (smaller than Westinghouse). My plan was to organize a half-dozen companies into a cooperative venture, creating one office equipped with a Copyflo to serve them all. I never was able to go through with my plan, but the time I spent on it drew me closer to the company and certainly gave me a better understanding of its operations—and a better reason for holding on to the stock, regardless of its bid-and-asked fluctuations.

Since this book is predicated on my belief that my "procedure" will prove very profitable to the average investor, you may protest that you haven't the time nor talent to go into a situation as thoroughly as I have. That point may have some validity. However, there are other means at your disposal. You can enlist the aid of your broker or pay a bit more attention to management reports. The following is quoted from the 1958 annual report of Haloid Xerox. Read it carefully; I am sure I did.

Tenth Anniversary of Xerography. 1958 marked the tenth anniversary of our entry into the field of xerography, for it was in 1948 that we acquired exclusive world rights to the basic Carlson patents issued following the invention of the process. This past decade has been one of vigorous research in an effort to gain mastery of this revolutionary new way of creating images with light and electricity. In the beginning, our xerographic products were elementary, hand-operated machines. Now we are introducing more sophisticated and valuable automatic products which make documentary copies of very high quality.

This year marks the threshold, we believe, of a new era in the growth of xerography and of Haloid Xerox. The xerography art has substantially matured, and therefore the next decade will be one of engineering developments while the process is applied to the many applications and markets where it will be useful. During the next few years, we expect to introduce several significant new machines, such as new copying devices, microfilm enlargers, computer printers. A continuing flow of xerographic products is anticipated for many years to come.

We approach this threshold buttressed by a dedicated organization imbued with the philosophy of pioneering, of growth, of willingness to accept risk and to search for new ways of engineering, manufacturing, selling, and financing.

Two other quotes from the same report should be carefully noted: "A number of new xerographic machines have been announced or are in such an advanced state of development that we are certain to announce them in 1959," and "During the next decade, we anticipate that the rate at which new products will be brought into the market will be considerably increased." Many clues were available to anyone interested enough to look for them that would give the alert analyst a better yardstick to evaluate the market value of Haloid Xerox. Right along, the consensus of opinion among important services was (and you heard it almost everywhere), "It's a good stock, a wonderful company, but it's selling much too high." All of which was not exactly encouraging to this writer whose holdings now represented a major portion of his portfolio. One popular service actually predicted in June 1959 (while praising the company), that its stock would decline 20 percent over the next five-year period. When this report was shown to me, I was not disturbed. Obviously, I commented, "they" had used an ordinary slide-rule to calculate Haloid Xerox' earnings over the past five or more years and projected earnings, as well, and multiplied the resultant figure with an "ordinary" P/E ratio. I use the word "ordinary" since I contended at that time, as well as today, that some companies need "extraordinary" analysis and I held steadfastly to my belief that Haloid Xerox was an extraordinary company.

In the spring of 1960, an atomic bomb was quietly dropped on the copy-machine industry—the Xerox 914 was unveiled. The full significance of its entrance into the office-machine industry was about to be unfolded in a number of directions

—all leading to the same conclusion, as far as the Wall Street analyst is concerned.

I examined the product itself; I used it and compared it with competition. I learned the demand for the 914 was far and above what management expected; its performance, its ease of operation, its ability to print multiple copies of high quality on ordinary paper, automatically and at low cost, greatly impressed me, as I am sure it did all who witnessed it. So much for a quick product analysis (which I recommend to all who investigate the merits of a prospective stock purchase).

I then examined the statements of the management. Let me list a few that I found pertinent (from the 1960 annual report):

> Xerox Corporation is the new name chosen for our Company. We shall recommend it to the shareholders for approval at the Annual Meeting. There is a fundamental and compelling reason for the recommendation. In 1961 more than 75% of our sales and a still higher percentage of our earnings will come from xerographic products. This is a revolutionary change from the situation a few years ago when the Haloid Company became Haloid Xerox Inc. At that time, sales of our photographic and xerographic products were about equal, and the name was changed to reflect the full scope of our business by adding the valuable trademark XEROX. In view of the revolution in our affairs during the last several years, and because our xerographic business will become even more important proportionately, we believe that XEROX should stand alone in our Company name. It will add to the powerful impact of this vital signature in our advertising and will more *precisely reveal our major field* [author's italics]. Since the 55-year-old name "Haloid" is widely known and respected in the photographic and photocopy industries, we will henceforth describe this part of our business as the Haloid Photo Division of XEROX Corporation.

. . . we were producing machines (the 914) at a rate nearly 50% greater at the end of the year than we had anticipated. . . . the number of orders taken during the first nine months of the Xerox 914's commercial life was substantially more than we had thought possible. . . . the average use for the machines installed has been much higher than our projections. . . . During 1960 we began construction of a new building for making xerographic developers. Our plans for this project were moved ahead about a year, because the placement of Xerox 914 machines has created a much greater demand for these materials than we had forecast. . . . We have expanded our rented facilities to increase the production of the Xerox 914 and another new product for engineering drawing reproduction, the Copyflo 1824. However, these rented facilities are not adequate, and we will begin construction of a machine manufacturing plant at Webster, New York, in the Spring of 1961. . . . During the year, Haloid Xerox played a part in the development of a prototype "Speed Mail" system, in cooperation with others. The system, which has been tested by the Post Office Department, permits transmission of "mail" between cities without physical transportation of the letter itself. The Speed Mail Letter, received at a post office in the normal manner, is inserted in special equipment which opens the envelope, scans and transmits in seconds the images on the letter to the receiving post office. At destination, the letter is reconstructed as a light beam and reproduced by xerography, as an exact duplicate of the original. It is automatically resealed in an envelope and delivered in the usual way. The original letter is automatically destroyed after transmission, thus preserving the privacy of the mails.

And there is an additional quote with reference to Rank Xerox.

During the past year Rank-Xerox Limited, our affiliate abroad, jointly owned with The Rank Organisation, made steady strides forward in a number of important areas. In a very real sense, xerography has, through the efforts of Rank Xerox, now come of age as a world-wide process. Rank Xerox Limited is today an expanding enterprise, manufacturing in England and distributing xerographic equipment and supplies to many parts of the world. . . . The Rank Xerox 14 has already been displayed at shows and fairs in London, Hanover, Paris, Amsterdam, and Zurich—and has met with a gratifying enthusiastic reception everywhere. . . . the progress already made is most heartening and augurs well for the future of xerography and its usefulness throughout the world.

As we review these statements, I am sure you will agree with me that all were very bullish, excepting one important factor, and I must confess it was very bearish indeed. That was Xerox's unbelievable high price/earnings ratio. High-ratio stocks were, of course, discounting the future, but were some discounting the hereafter as well? To determine whether the present P/E ratio is too high or too low for an individual company is a most difficult one, particularly where an extremely high-ratio stock is concerned.

To this aspect of the Xerox story, I should like to quote from an address by Mr. Joseph C. Wilson before The New York Society of Security Analysts in December 1961.

How high the moon? This venerable question, until a decade ago, or perhaps even five years, meant one thing; a kind of ironic implication that starry eyed visionaries were assaying the unattainable. Does it mean the same thing today? Of course not. We and the Soviets are mightily straining to reach the moon—but already our eyes are on more distant stars. Yet *Forbes Magazine*, in September, used that headline for an article about Xerox. The reference, of course, was to its stock's price earnings ratio which, the writer said, was the highest of any listed on the New York Stock Exchange. We have not done any research to confirm this assertion. Let us just accept the fact that it is on the high side.

I suppose my task today is not to justify the ratio, product as it is of the myriad judgments of a free market, but to illuminate the factors which probably cause it. Alas, it seems to me, the emphasis should be on the somewhat obscure elements in our situation rather than to say again the things all of you can read in published material.

Let us start the illumination by searching for a somewhat firmer base. What is Xerox' price-earnings ratio? Price is definite enough. On November 20, the quotation was over $130 which is over 180 times our reported per share earnings for the year 1960, but of course, you already know that our nine months earnings in 1961 are up over 90 percent compared with the same period a year ago. For the year as a whole they will probably be almost double those of 1960 because our earnings trend is improving rather rapidly. This is shown by the sharp increase in our sales and profits since the first quarter. Fourth quarter sales will probably be 50 percent higher than first quarter sales with net profits showing a greater proportionate gain. Thus, historical earnings for Xerox do not mean very much.

I would like to remind you also not to look at our profit per share without thinking, at least, of our cash flow per share, because our charges for patent amortization and depreciation of leased equipment are a very heavy drain on our reported profit but they are deductible for tax and provide large sources of cash. Thus, although our price earnings ratio may be one hundred times 1961 earnings, it is rather important to note that our price to cash flow per share ratio will be about thirty-five times. This reflects an almost unique relation of non-cash charges to profit.

It is important also to remember that the great increase in our business this year comes primarily from rentals which means that a greater share of our sales and profits are being deferred into subsequent years, the "quality" of our earning power is changing for the better as astute observers like Anton Rice, of Spencer Trask, have been suggesting.

However, no one, I suppose, even considers Xerox stock now unless he is primarily concerned with future earnings. . . . To bring you some comprehension of this future, I suppose, you must have answers to two fundamental questions. One—is this company working in a field of large enough potential to continue indefinitely its planned rate of growth of 20 percent? The second one is a corollary. Are we competent to reach this potential if it is there?

There is evidence to suggest that the answer to the second question is yes.

Mr. Wilson continued with some very significant projections that had a profound impact on me as a shareholder.

Xerox entered the [office copying] market with our 914 in the Spring of 1960, about 20 months ago. . . . By the end of 1961 Xerox will have about 2 percent of the machines in the market, but our machines will produce over 25 percent of the copies. *On 2 percent of the machines, I repeat, over 25 percent of the copies will be made.* This is an achievement of which we are proud indeed for this is a market studded with formidable competitors. . . . What do we plan to do during the next five years with this carefully tuned instrument?

On March 2, 1957, at a meeting of Xerox people I said with extreme naiveté, that after five years the company's sales would be triple what they were then and that its margin of profit on those sales would be greater. During the next year this prediction was repeated publicly to groups of analysts in several cities. It was a hazardous thing to do. Many people advised against doing it and undoubtedly they were right. It happens, however, that in 1956, the year before the prediction, our sales were a little less than 24 million. In 1962, five years later, we are confident that they will more than triple that figure. In 1956, our ratio of net income before taxes to sales was a little less than 12.5 percent. In 1961, it will be over 18 percent and in 1962 we believe more than 20 percent, despite the great increase in rentals as a proportion of the total and in depreciation and amortization as charges reducing net income. Having survived this hazardous forecasting once, I choose to stretch my luck by saying forthrightly to you, who deserve to know, what we plan to do by the end of 1966. . . . If we have been right, business will be earning more than three times as much profit in five years and its cash flow may be as much as one dollar of each four dollars of sales. Our cash flow will almost equal our sales in 1961. . . .

On October 22 of this year another growth company, our respected competitor, Minnesota Mining, released a study of business and government. It said in part that American business turns out paper work at about the same rate as the government—an estimated 25,000 papers or documents per year per employee; and the creating of business records, including wages for clerical time, is estimated to cost industry $100 billion a year. If you add an estimate for government and another for the world outside the United States, you describe a market of perhaps $200 billion annually. This is our field. It is our potential and it is growing with great dynamism. Should our objective be to attain one-half of one percent of it?—a billion dollars? Why not?

"A billion dollars? Why not?" So concluded Mr. Wilson's address. I want you to make a particular note of this "billion dollars" in the light of a previous comment of mine that I found Mr. Wilson a man who was prone to understate things and (I am not being facetious) at a time when Xerox's total operating revenues leaped to a record high of $61 million.

A month later we celebrated the New Year, 1962, with the usual enthusiasm of the bulls who were predicting fantastic new highs for the Dow Jones averages. Notwithstanding, the market began to slide: Blue Monday and a few Black Fridays tumbled prices to half and less their previous highs. IBM dropped from $600 to $300. It appeared to me that Xerox was trying to resist the decline, but it too followed suit, breaking below $90, from about $160. Had I missed the boat? Once again I was being advised, "Sell at least half," "You will be able to buy it back for less," and so on. Some of my friends did sell, but they never got back into Xerox.

Why did I stubbornly refuse to sell a single share of Xerox at that time? There was certainly enough pressure to do so. My holdings (at the top) were worth over $200,000, which is more than I dreamed I would ever be worth. Yet, I had sound reasons *not* to sell. Go along with me carefully to learn the secret of what little success I have had with various securities.

1. When a stock goes down, I try to ascertain the reason for its action; I follow the same procedure when it goes up. Was anything wrong with the Xerox picture? Indeed not! 1961 earnings per share were up over 140 percent, and from what I gathered, 1962 earnings per share would show a greater than a 100 percent increase. In simple arithmetic, 1962 earnings per share would likely be four to five times 1960, just two years earlier.

2. What about the future? Had Xerox reached its peak? On the contrary, Xerox seemed to be scratching the surface. Their research and development expeditures kept increasing at a robust rate, something like 9 to 10 percent of total operating revenues. I watched with pride the expanded use of the advertising columns of *The New York Times* seeking more and more engineers, physicists, marketing, and sales help. I had great confidence that management knew what it was doing.

3. Despite the turmoil in the market, my wife and I left for a three-month European vacation early in June, thus avoiding some bad days, since the daily shipboard Wall Street bulletins, when we did get them, made no mention of Xerox. On my arrival in London, I had the pleasure of visiting Mr. John Davis, the Chairman of Rank Organisations, who is also

a director of Xerox. It was a very cordial visit; Mr. Davis offered to have a limousine take us out to the Rank Xerox plant at Mitcheldean. Without asking any questions that might prove embarrassing, I could not detect any sign of misgivings about the future of Xerox and Rank Xerox.

4. What about my personal feelings at seeing a good part of my paper profits melting away? And how did I feel to have some of my best friends keep telling me, "Paper profits don't mean a thing until you take them." And more of my close friends kept saying, "I told you so." There is, of course, no reason for celebrating your paper losses, but note—and this is the most important part of my philosophy—that an investor's personal emotions should have nothing whatever to do with determining his decision to buy or sell. I could find no bearishness in the Xerox picture, so I had no reason to sell. And thus I had the good fortune to weather the 1962 break in the market.

To "buy" a stock is not enough; one must continue to *concentrate* on the operations of the company, its management, and its potential, rather than worry about the daily fluctuations of its market price and one's own profit or loss position. I continued to write to Mr. Wilson offering a few suggestions or observations about a Xerox product or service. I received some very warm replies addressing me as "Dear Sam" and signed, "Cordially, Joe," always thanking me for my interest and sometimes complimenting me on my thinking. I continued with my suggestions, one of which I am proud of: I named the facsimile system "Long Distance Xerography."

Making suggestions comes naturally to an advertising man, as well as studying a company and its products, and as my stake in Xerox increased in value, so did my interest. But I must point out that this kind of thinking does not come naturally to most investors. On the contrary, too many stockholders see their profits grow larger and their interest in the company wanes. Their attention is diverted to thoughts of getting out; they cannot stand prosperity and decide to sell while other astute investors get in.

It is a far wiser policy to look for clues as to why a stock is making new highs. In the case of Xerox, there were many bullish clues available to anyone interested enough to look for them. (Similar clues are available in all stocks, if you dig for them.)

Previously, I described Mr. Wilson as a man prone to understate; so let us examine some of his "understatements." They certainly sounded like gross exaggerations when they were made.

"In five years our sales will be tripled" (1957). Actually, 1962 sales of $105 million more than quadrupled 1957 sales of $26 million. Net income per share went from $.09 to $.71. The next understatement: "In five years our cash flow will almost equal our sales this year" (1961). This indeed was an amazing prediction, especially when it was given to a group of hard-hearted veteran analysts. However, it did not take five years; in three years, by the end of 1964, cash flow was $83 million as against $63 million in *sales* in 1961. Many other clues were available in the quarterly progress reports on new products and market and research developments; and in all these reports, it appeared to me that management was understating. With my own brand of mathematics, I upped my bullish expectations and continued to hold on to all my Xerox.

But not everyone thinks alike. At the annual meeting in

May 1964, Mr. Wilson told the assembled shareholders that Xerox was developing a new product that was costing the company $40 million. A hush fell over the audience, particularly since Mr. Wilson noted that this was twice the sum spent developing the Xerox 813. I recall discussing this with some of my fellow shareholders after the meeting. Some wondered if Xerox management was biting off more than it could chew. I was confident that management knew what it was doing, and I believe the Street agreed with me, for the stock rose to $130 per share, obviously unfazed by the expense of the new Xerox product. The unveiling was announced for October 14 at the New York Hilton. Excitement filled the air. The press and the analysts were invited, and I was there.

But a funny thing happened on the way to the Hilton. Xerox dropped ten points the day before, which prompted Mr. Wilson's opening remarks: "I cannot understand you New York boys; here we are presenting the biggest thing in our history, and you tell us we're worth some $200 million less than we were yesterday." And he went on unfolding the story of the Xerox 2400 with such superb understatementship that I was impelled to compliment him. Simultaneously, C. Peter McColough, then executive vice president of operations, introduced the Xerox 2400 in Chicago, and John H. Dessauer, executive vice president of research and engineering, served as chief company spokesman in Washington.

Notwithstanding, the stock tumbled another twenty-five points in a very short period of time, midst a barrage of bearish statements. One issue of the *Wall Street Transcript* contained a half-dozen reports citing ever lower support levels. Coincidentally, IBM announced it would enter the copying machine field via Harris Intertype; many analysts attributed the weakness in Xerox to this coming competition. A number of pros asked me for an opinion, especially in the light of IBM's anticipated formidable competition. I could find no one to agree with my common-sense analysis:

1. If the Street was right, then the $40 million in research and development spent on the new 2400 was a colossal miscalculation by Xerox management.

2. No one in his right mind could think that about Joe and his staff.

3. Did the analysts understand the 2400 and its potential? Definitely *not!* How else could they have been so wrong? Here was the 2400 designed to "seek a share of the $3.5 billion market estimated for office reproduction of all kinds." "The system, unique among high-speed reproduction devices," was "faster than copying" and "simpler than duplicating or printing."

4. I examined the product thoroughly. I happen to be a typist myself, a fairly good one. In the Xerox 2400 (which required no skill whatever to operate) I recognized an automaton that could produce several hundred copies before I could adjust a stencil into my typewriter and start typing. Its value in time- and labor-saving alone was incalculable.

5. What about IBM? I forecast an early severance of its deal with Harris Intertype. I understood that this was not the first attempt by IBM to enter the copying market. I never underestimated the power of IBM and the quality of its management; I reasoned they would never spend millions to develop a product that would be second best, and from what I was able to ascertain about the Harris Intertype product, Xerox shareholders had no cause to worry.

And thus I continued holding all my Xerox.

The following year, 1965 (which the company previously announced they would need for "training, indoctrination and full-scale production, and to undertake, publicly, exhaustive field tests of the 2400") was a good one, marketwise; the stock doubled, evidently reflecting the progress the 2400 was making. This progress was confirmed to me in an indirect manner. A friend of mine went to Chicago to update his report on Addressograph; on his return, he told me they were very much concerned about the 2400. I interpreted this bit of news as indicating that ADR salesmen were returning with the tidings that some of their prospects were waiting for the Xerox 2400.

All of which brings us up to the summer of 1966—the big break that dropped the Dow Jones averages from close to 1,000 to about 740. Many stocks were selling at one-half their highs; the blue chips, the glamor favorites, the high and the low fell victims to an avalanche of selling. Xerox resisted the pressure remarkably well, even going against the trend. But it too buckled and finally collapsed. While enjoying a sunny vacation in Italy, I read about the block of 100,000 shares of Xerox that crossed the tape (early in August) at $200—a $20 million sale that still holds the record as the largest single sale on the Big Board. By the time I returned in mid-September, the stock had broken another thirty points. Then in one week (it should be spelled w-e-a-k) it fell another 42 points, and actually touched 125 and a fraction.

Had I missed the boat for sure, this time? I did not think so. In my book, Xerox was not only a growth stock but a super growth stock. Of course, it was at the mercy of a new breed of performance-minded mutual fund managements. But was there anything frightening beyond the Xerox horizon to account for such an about-face? None that I could detect. On the contrary, I learned about a half-dozen new Xerox products being readied for the market. More importantly, it was my understanding from public announcements that 1967 research and development was budgeted at over $50 million, and—please note this—at least half this amount was for products *other than* xerography. I held on to all my Xerox.

chapter fourteen

C. Peter McColough: A continuation of the Xerox story

I have called C. Peter McColough "Peter" as long as I have known him and so has everyone else. It is more than a hark-back to the old Haloid days when every factory worker greeted their boss, Joseph C. Wilson, "Hi, Joe"; Joe, John, Sol, Kent, and Peter were all members of that one family. I have sensed this strong family attachment through the years; such informality has much to do, I am sure, with the unprecedented success of the Xerox Corporation. I felt very flattered they included me: "Sam, you are one of us."

To say that Joe was the head of the family and the one man most responsible for the development of a small, obscure company into a multi-billion dollar corporation is an understatement. To say that Peter, the new head of the family, had a tough act to follow is equally an understatement.

137

I first learned about Peter in a letter I received from Joe Wilson, then president of Haloid Xerox, Inc., Products for Xerography and Photography. It was dated May 1, 1959. As a small stockholder, I was so impressed with the Xerox 24″ Copyflo which had recently been introduced. It enlarged a microfilm about 2 inches square into a blueprint 24 by 36 inches on plain paper in about six seconds; I was considering leasing one at $40,000 per year and subleasing it to smaller corporations who had less need for the Copyflo on a yearly basis. I quote from his letter:

> I shall leave this correspondence with Mr. C. P. McColough, Manager of Marketing, the young man in our organization who perhaps has had more to do with the establishment of our own Processing Labs than anyone else. He knows this phase of the business far better than I. If you would like to spend some time with him here in Rochester, please make a mutually convenient date.

After Joe Wilson's maiden speech before the New York Society of Security Analysts on December 4, 1961, broke up and the crowds hurried back to their ticker tapes, quite by accident I was invited to join two men who were taking a taxi uptown. It was Peter who invited me. The other gentleman was Paul Garrett, a public relations man. We probably chatted about the weather or the cold roast beef they served for lunch, but I do recall an aura of success that lingered on after the meeting. The feeling was genuine and not a figment of my imagination. My entire wealth at the time was hardly six figures, but I had fortunately learned to distinguish genuine enthusiasm from the phony or prefabricated kind. (Which is why I refrained from buying certain stocks that sounded too bullish; and I avoided big losses, too.)

Through the years that followed, I got to know Peter very well, although we were never in close contact. I made a suggestion to him every now and then; and once, when I had a slight argument with their advertising agent who claimed he suggested L D X (Long Distance Xerography), I casually asked Peter: "Who gave you LDX?" and he promptly said "You did, Sam." On a few occasions he greeted me: "Hi, Sam, are you coming up to Rochester? Chicago? Los Angeles?" And each time, I would say "God willing."

It was in Chicago, that Xerox held its annual meeting, May 19, 1966. That was the day Joe surprised us by announcing (while we were having lunch) that Peter was named president. It did not come as a complete surprise to me as I had known that Joe was shifting a lot of the work, little by little, on to the young man who was manager of marketing just seven years ago. On the way to congratulate Peter, I met John Dessauer (director and head of research, who was the one who took Joe Wilson to evaluate an invention by Chester Carlson). Said John: "Sam, you knew we were grooming Peter for the job for five years."

When I caught up with Peter, he was having lunch with his wife Virginia and a few of the directors. "Congratulations, Peter" I said, "but I did not expect this for another year or two." "Thanks, Sam" he said "but, nothing has changed."

"Nothing has changed." Three simple words. A seemingly casual statement but one of great significance to me—as an indication of the character of the man who was just elevated to the presidency of a company that is considered to be one of the Great Success Stories of the century. Knowing Peter as I do, I have attached even greater importance to his words. They signified the humbleness of the man, that he considered himself just another member of the family and that the family was doing well and would continue doing well.

Two years later, on May 16, 1968, C. Peter McColough became chief executive officer of Xerox; you might add the "head of the family," for Joe was easing out of his heavy schedule with thoughts of retirement, confident that the family was in good hands. "The young fellows" Joe said at the 1971 annual meeting "are heading for a five to ten billion dollar company. We will keep an eye on them." (My mind went back and I am sure Joe's did, too, to his remarks a decade earlier, before the New York Society of Security Analysts, "Should our objective be—a billion dollars? Why not?" It seemed like pure fantasy then when total revenues hit a record high of $61 million.)

I wonder if my readers could put themselves in Peter's place at the time he became head of the family. I know it would scare the hell out of me; I am quite sure that Peter felt that way too, for a reason that is not too apparent. Here we are dealing with a company that rose from obscurity to a billion dollar corporation in a single decade; the only company to do so in the history of American industry. It would be somewhat similar to being made coach of the Los Angeles basketball team, the Lakers, who had not lost a game in several years. Where do we go from here?

The finest tribute I can pay to Peter is to report that he took it in stride, as I knew he would—but not without trepidation. In the fall of 1968, Peter (with a hand-shake) tried to buy C.I.T. Financial (assets $3.7 billion) for $1.5 billion of Xerox stock. It did not meet with popular approval. Instead, he bought Scientific Data Systems (assets $113 million) for $900 million in Xerox stock. It was very costly. I casually said to Peter some time later "We paid a heluva price for

SDS" and he added quite casually "We needed it, Sam." To *Forbes* magazine he said: "It was absolutely essential for Xerox to have a computer capability to reach the objectives we have set for the 70s.

As *Forbes* put it, Xerox was entering "The McColough Era" successor to the "Joe Wilson-Sol Linowitz" Era. Personally, I would say it was a *continuation* of the Joe Wilson-Sol Linowitz era. Peter's job was not only to maintain Xerox's position in the copying and duplicating field—what a tough act to follow—but to move significantly into computers, education, medicine, and communications. And there had to be a confrontation with Goliath—I.B.M.—on the way. How good Peter was with a slingshot no one knew.

He needed help, much help, and like every young father made plans for a larger family. In retrospect, I do not hesitate to call Peter's accomplishment a classic example of corporate planned parenthood at its best. From Ford he took Archie McCardell and Jacob Goldman as his research head. (I remember reading that Jack Goldman had a much bigger R & D budget at Xerox than he had at Ford. Xerox's R & D budget, under John Dessauer, from its infancy was always large, about 10 percent of sales. I always referred to it as Xerox's secret weapon.) He took Joe Flavin from IBM for planning and finance. Another financial planning genius, Sanford Kaplan, came from SDS. Bob Haigh from Standard Oil(Ohio) headed Xerox's million education group. Raymond Hay who did not join Xerox until 1961 became head of business products, which at the time accounted for 83 percent of Xerox revenues. Bill Souders was manager of product planning at the time Peter became boss; today he is senior vice president and chief staff officer of the corporation.

I might be overlooking some of the newer men who are

making good contributions to Xerox's growth so I apologize for their omission. They know who they are and they know, too, that Peter knows. But with your permission, Peter, I would like to say "Hello" to your old secretary and treasurer, Kent Damon. A Xerox man if there ever was one. I don't know if you realize it, but Kent may easily be the hardest working and most popular man on your team: he signs all the dividend checks that keep rolling in—in increasing amounts.

To say that Peter's family gets along admirably and is doing a fine job is a massive understatement which has not escaped the eyes of the investment public. Wall Street has its own yardstick in measuring a company's accomplishments.

On November 22, 1971, we heard the shocking news that Joseph Chamberlain Wilson suffered a heart attack and died. He was having lunch at the time in New York state's Governor Rockefeller's home. It took many months for most of us to realize that Joe was gone; though his philosophy, principles, precepts, and his appreciation of human values in business as well as in society shall ever remain as part of Xerox family life.

I happily recall the last annual meeting Joe attended in May of that year. I had made a short talk pointing out that the big money managers were paying a much higher P/E for Xerox than for IBM. I concluded that "this is the highest tribute that can be paid to Xerox management and its board of directors."

After the meeting, midst handshakes, as busy as he was greeting his friends, Joe found time to say "Thanks, Sam, for those fine remarks." That was the last time I saw him.

C. Peter McColough became chairman of the board and Archie McCardell was named president. I sent Peter a note of congratulations; I received in return a typical "Dear Sam" thank you note adding, "Thanks, Sam, for your continued support." A rather humble remark. But that's Peter as I know him. Certainly, I know of no one more worthy of the support of a stockholder. I would like to add a few quotes to give my readers a better insight into Peter's character as well as his philosophy and plans.

Some of the following quotes come from the September 1972 issue of *Nation's Business,* in answer to certain questions:

> *Q.:* What would you say is Xerox' greatest strength as a company?
>
> I think that it's probably our aggressive spirit of innovation in depth—not assets like patents or manufacturing plants or money. We believe willingness to try new things should be general in the company, and not just connected with research and development.
>
> *Q.:* What is the company's greatest weakness, if any?
>
> It is very hard for me to tell you what that would be. I think the greatest fear we have about weakness is that as we grow, as we're already very large, we will get the big company syndrome—and we will become slow and cautious, people will be afraid to make mistakes, and we will build up barriers and fail to communicate.
>
> There is no more important thing to me in my job than trying to do what I can to prevent that. As you get bigger and older, you very often want to play it safe. You're trying to guarantee your security. . . . We want people to get ahead not because they know the rules but because they are thinking. . . . We try not to have some of the trappings of a big, staid company. ˙. . or get into all the hierarchy of distinctions . . . like the

key to the executive washroom. . . . no executive dining rooms . . . we want our people to mix . . . we try to do a lot of other things to keep the company informal.

We are "first-name" right through the company. There are few people who don't call me Peter—no old-timers, anyway. Around the office, now, more people call me Mr. McColough, but I think that's because they're new and I'm getting older.

February 1973 . . . Our growth objectives for the next seven years are tough, mighty tough. In fact, the objectives which we are setting are almost unprecedented in the history of American business. . . .

You just don't do the difficult things without some pressure. . . .

If we are going to have our goals, we are going to have the pressures . . . it's exciting . . . I think most of our people welcome both.

Another example of original thinking and genuine concern about Xerox employees:

I have a rule that anybody who has been with Xerox for eight years cannot be dismissed without my personal written approval.

If we have taken so many years of his life, we have a responsibility to him. We have to learn to take a good hard look at a guy after two or three years of employment. If there is any question about his ability, about whether this is the place he should plan to make a career, I think we ought to ask him at a young age to go some place else when he hasn't already invested a major part of his life in the company.

In my capacity as an investment adviser (to a very few clients) but mostly for myself in evaluating a company's potential, my first concern has always been management, as well as my second and third concern, to be truthful. Actually I owe my good fortune (my large Xerox holdings) to the fact that my analyses were sound right from the start, 21 years ago, when all I put into Haloid was $3,000—for a very good reason, it was practically all I could afford to invest. But I have always been puzzled, Peter, by the take-it-for-granted attitude on the part of many of our fellow stockholders at our annual meetings. It's always a happy get-together, of course. There was applause when the Xerox 1200 computer print-out system and the Xerox 6500 Color Copier were shown; but when Jack Goldman mentioned Xerox had spent a quarter of a billion on R & D and Archie McCardell stated Xerox earnings would reach three billion, there was hardly a murmur. I am not finding fault with our stockholders and I don't even know if you on the other side of the dais even noticed this take-it-for-granted attitude. We are spoiled, definitely, and expect more miracles from our management.

The public is spoiled, too. A child can push a button on a Xerox copier and receive 60 clean copies in a minute and each copy will be as sharp as the original. Little does the public—and most of our stockholders—realize, for example, that the Xerox 4000 (which is substantially increasing Xerox revenues) has 1,900 parts. How much hard work and how many millions was spent to develop it, I don't know. And how many millions were spent to train the Xerox technical representatives who must service the copier in the place where the customer uses it. He must know what all the 1,900 parts are, what they do, and how to keep them doing it at top efficiency.

The Xerox story and it's continuation extoll management, and rightly so, and fittingly highlight The Wonderful World of Wall Street. Like "Ol' Man River" XEROX management keeps rolling along, at a growth rate unprecedented for a multi-billion dollar corporation.

chapter fifteen

Summing up

Let's confront the question you had in your mind when you picked up this book: Is there *really* money to be made in the stock market? My answer is yes! Despite the proliferation of ill-informed parrots, go-go Khans, and Asses along Wall Street, there *is* still money to be made in the stock market. If you understand that this money must be worked for—that it will not accrue to you for taking tips and guessing right on hot issues but must be earned by careful evaluation and constant management—I can virtually guarantee your success.

Master the three Es to the best of your ability. Alone, or with the aid of your broker or a proven investment adviser, explore, examine, and evaluate any stock before you commit yourself. Concentrate on management and potential growth. Use your head! Never buy a stock because you "want to be in the market and make some money."

Choose an industry with better than average growth potential. Choose a company whose management has shown that it has the imagination to recognize this potential growth and the competence to achieve it. Compare the accomplishments of any company that interests you to those of its competitors.

When you decide upon a stock whose prospects you evaluate to be basically bullish, invest in it to the extent you can *comfortably*. It is foolish and tragic to overinvest. You cannot manage an investment properly if your financial future is threatened by every market fluctuation.

Repeat the evaluation process periodically for each stock you own. Assess how well the stock is doing in terms of what it is capable of doing, *not* in terms of what you wish it would do. This advice is invaluable whenever you are tempted to take a profit—or a loss. Every stock revolves on its own axis, an axis I call the pivot line. You have probably never heard of a pivot line under this or any other name; nor has it ever received the attention it merits. But it is of prime importance, as you shall see.

Most investors quite naturally focus their attention on the price they paid for a stock. Such an investor may not have a name for it, but that initial purchase *price pivot line* becomes the axis around which all his calculations revolve. If he has a profit, it is measured from the pivot line; if he has a loss, it too is measured from the pivot line. The fallacy of this line of thinking is that a stock's current pivot line may have nothing at all to do with the original purchase price.

For example, suppose you paid $100 for a certain stock some months or years ago that is currently selling around $65 to $75 a share, in a trading range of ten points. Thus, the current pivot line should be assessed at around $70. As far as this stock is concerned, this $70 pivot line is the axis about which the trading revolves. Whether you want to take your loss or buy more, you must completely forget the price you paid (the market evidently has long since forgotten it) and make your decision based on where you believe the stock is going from the present pivot line. To this decision you must bring all the information and evaluation you can gather about your company's operations. When you can forget your personal position and evaluate the stock on its own merits, your ability to do the right thing will be immeasurably advanced.

This kind of pivot line evaluation is just as important on the profit-taking side as it is on the loss side. For example, I originally bought Xerox (Haloid) at around $30 a share. After a trying year or two, it was selling above $100. Had I focused my attention on a $30 pivot line, there is no doubt in my mind that I would have taken my profit somewhere along the line. However, when I evaluated the stock on the $100 pivot line (and later, at higher points) and found that the company was still moving in the ways that had caused me to choose it initially—management was performing extraordinarily well, research and development were exemplary, in short, all the bullish factors still existed—there was every reason to believe that not only could the stock sustain its present price level, it could very well exceed it.

I cannot stress enough the importance of evaluating each stock from time to time without involving yourself emotionally in the assessment. You must forget whatever profits or losses you may have in order to do this. It may require some additional homework (research), but it is well worth the effort. Do not become discouraged when you learn that corporate executives and registered representatives cannot give you as much time and as thorough reports as are available to professional analysts. First, you have access to professional analysts if you want it; and second, with a bit of imagination, from all the information available to you in company reports and press releases, you can piece together a pretty good picture of what is going on in *your* companies.

Plan a portfolio of stocks that balance each other. Do not depend on one or two stocks, no matter how well they are doing. I strongly recommend that you add some conservative issues to balance the more volatile growth stocks in your portfolio. For these I choose low P/E ratio stocks that pay good dividends and stand up better than growth stocks in declining markets. Remember to review *all* your stocks often, and weed out any issues that do not meet your standards for holding on to them.

Hand in hand with planning a balanced portfolio goes the advice not to spread yourself too thin. Hold only the number of stocks that you can follow and understand. Remember, stocks are investments that must be *managed*.

Plan to be in the market over the long run. Occasionally, you will hear of a whiz kid who leaped into the market with $10,000 and out again in six months with $1 million. Personally, I don't believe that I am brilliant enough to be in exactly the right place for exactly the right length of time to make a killing, and I know perfectly well that I couldn't stand the emotional strain in any case! Moreover, for every whiz kid who lucks out, there are at least 100,000 suckers who lose their shirts.

Don't panic every time the market trembles. Remember, there are flood tides, ebb tides, and riptides, and your stocks are as subject to the inexorable laws of the marketplace as are anyone else's. If your original evaluations are sound and you continue to manage your portfolio scrupulously, your results will be profitable in the best sense of the word.

Index

A

Adviser, 44–48, 69
  fee, 45–48
  portfolio manager, 53–54
Advisory service to institutional clients, 48, 69
Airlines, 34–36
  competition, 35
  rates fixed by government, 35, 36
Analyst, 66–68
Arbitrage, 114

B

B/A (broker-adviser), 45
Balanced portfolio, 150
B.C. (Beauty and Comfort) sales plan, 35
Bear market, 15–16, 17, 18
  brokerage houses, 42
  broker's advice, 69
  making money in, 19–20
Best & Co., 24–26
Broker, 31–39
  adviser, 45

Broker—*Cont.*
  "big producer," 44
  service, 43, 45–46
Brokerage commission, 26–28
  adviser's fee, 45–47
  negotiated, 26
  price-fixed, 38–39, 56
  rate structure, 45, 48, 56
Brokerage houses
  losses, 32–33
  profit, 37
  research and advisory personnel, 42
  service, 26–29, 45
Bull market, 15, 18
  broker's advice, 68
  stockpiling losses, 17
  switching, 20

C

Chain-store operation, 37–38
Chartered Financial Analyst, 67
Commission; *see* Brokerage commission
Company
  evaluation of, 7–9

Company—*Cont.*
  management, 8
  vital statistics, 8
Conglomerate, 14–15
Con man, 79–81
Copyflo, 120–21
Customer's man, 47, 68

D

Davis, John, 130–31
Dessauer, John H., 133, 139, 141
Discount house, 42
Dow Jones averages, 32

E–F

Electronic Data Systems, 32
Evaluation of company, 7–9
  stock worth, 147–49
Financial Analysts Federation, 66–67
Full disclosure, 62

G–H

Gambling, 59
Glamour stock, 62–63
Goldman, Jacob (Jack), 141, 145
Goodbody & Co., 33
Haloid Company, 43, 118, 120
  P/E ratio, 119
Haloid-Xerox Company, 120–23
  P/E ratio, 123
Harris Intertype, 133–34
How to Make Big Money in the Stock Market, 56

I

IBM, 133–34
Investment business, 1, 28
  mechanics of, 38, 48
  practice, 1–2
  research and advisory departments, 48
  theory, 1–2
Investor, 2
  gambling, 60
  professional, 2–3
  small, 23–29
Investors Overseas Services, 33

L

Ladies Home Journal, 51
le Boutelier, Phillip, 25
Levitz Furniture Company, 4–7
Ling, Temco, Vought, 33
Linowitz, Sol, 66, 141
Long Distance Xerography, 131, 139
Loss-taking, 87
Losses, 4, 11–17
  stockpiling, 4, 17

M

McColough, C. Peter, 133, 137–45
Management
  competence, 8
  customer relations, 25
  of investments, 51–58
  profits, 25
Market letter, 69
Memorex, 33
Mergers, 114
Merrill Lynch, Pierce Fenner & Smith, 33, 38
  chain-store operation, 37
  research, 48–49
Mutual funds, 27–28
  no-load funds, 28

N–O

Negotiated commission, 26
New York Society of Security Analysts, 66
New York Stock Exchange, 34
  examination of registered representatives, 68
No-load fund, 28
Odd-lot theory, 95

P

Parker, C. Reed, 67
Penn Central Railroad, 32
P/E ratio; *see* Price/earnings ratio
Pivot line, 148–49
Portfolio manager, 53–55
Price/earnings ratio, 15, 68
  Xerox, 126–27, 142

Price fixing, 38
Price pivot line, 148
Profit
    management responsibility for,
      24–25
    quick, 21
    squeeze, 35
Profit-taking, 85–87

R

Rank-Xerox Limited, 125–26, 130–31
Rate structure
    airlines, 35–36
    brokerage commissions, 45, 48, 56
Registered representative (RR), 27–
    28, 69; *see also* Broker
    adviser, 44
    as analyst, 68
Research man, 44, 66

S

Scientific Data Systems, 140–41
Sears Roebuck Company, 37–38
Securities and Exchange Commission,
    26
Security analyst, 66
Security business; *see* Investment busi-
    ness
Short selling, 19, 111–16
    amateurs, 114–15
    tax advantage, 113
Stock
    acquiring, 7

Stock—*Cont.*
    evaluation of worth, 8–9, 147–49
    P/E ratio, 150
Stock market, 7
    explanation for drop in, 16
    making money in, 147–51
    small investor
Stockpiling losses, 4
    bull market, 17
Switching, 20, 88–92
Syndicate, con men, 79

T

Technician, 44
Tip, 65–75
    adviser, 69
    reliable information, 73
Trone, Robert W., 48

U–X

University Computing, 33
Vanderbilt, Commodore, 112
Volatile stock, 16, 17, 19
    bull market, 18
Wall Street Journal, 17
Wilson, Joseph C., 66, 120, 126,
    128–29, 132–33, 137–42
Xerox Corporation, 52–53, 117–45
    employee relations, 144
    management, 144
    name change, 124
    price/earnings ratio, 126–27, 142